HALCYON *in the* HEBRIDES

HALCYON

in the

HEBRIDES

BOB ORRELL

Whittles Publishing

Published by
Whittles Publishing Ltd.,
Dunbeath,
Caithness, KW6 6EG,
Scotland, UK

www.whittlespublishing.com

ISBN 978-184995-040-4

Printed in Great Britain by Ashford Colour Press Ltd

For Patricia
who made the journey possible

CONTENTS

BY THE SAME AUTHOR

Amulet – *A Charm Restored and Sailed to the Western Isles*
Blowout
Saddle Tramp in the Lake District
Saddle Tramp in the Highlands
Saddle Tramp on the Isle of Man
Over the Fells
Lakeland Monuments
Best Guide to Ravenglass
Best Guide to Cumbrian Shows
Around and About Ennerdale
The Company History of Borderway Livestock Mart, Carlisle

ACKNOWLEDGEMENTS

Many anonymous local people took time to give me help and advice and tell me interesting stories during my wanderings – and to them, my grateful thanks.

Thanks also to Captain Arthur Manson; George Rich, ex-RYA Examiner; Stornoway Library; The Island Heritage Centre, Barra; Northern Lighthouse Board Archives; Andrew Mumford; Captain Ronnie Holmes; Stuart Miller; and a special thanks to Jean Thompson who kept a critical eye on the typescript.

Scottish Records very kindly gave permission for the use of lines from the song 'The Crinan Canal' by Alex MacKenzie from the CD *Highland Journey*.

Every effort has been made to trace copyright holders and to obtain permission for the use of copyright material. The publisher would be grateful if notified of any amendments that should be incorporated in future reprints or editions of this book.

Map and boat diagram by Louis Mackay Design and Illustration Ltd.

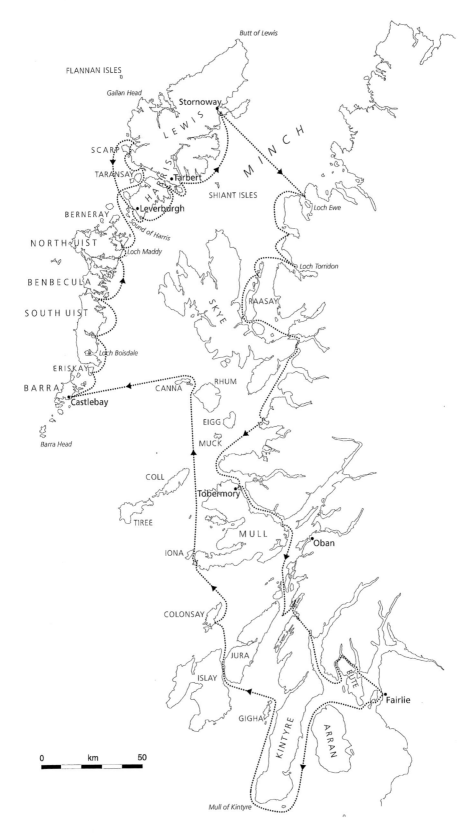

Route taken by Halcyon

1

A NUCLEAR SEA MONSTER – DR JAGO'S DREAM SHIP

The fast, out-going tide gurgled and hissed around the base of the fairway buoy marking the edge of the main shipping channel at the tail of the River Clyde, and I manoeuvred my yacht, *Halcyon*, close-in to read its name and check my position. A light wind had been blowing from the east for nearly a week, and a peculiarity of the Clyde weather was that an east wind invariably brought misty conditions with it. Since mid-morning visibility had varied from half a mile to barely being able to see the end of *Halcyon*'s bowsprit.

Straining to listen for the sound of engines or a foghorn, I shoved the engine into gear and was nosing across the channel when, through the murk, a sinister black mass surged towards me, pushing a wall of water in front of it. Distorted by the mist, it looked like a hideous sea monster that had escaped from the set of a horror movie and, rigid with shocked disbelief, I stared at it as it drew closer. Then rapid blasts on a ship's siren brought me to my senses, and as the thing began to take shape I realised it was the hull and conning tower of a nuclear submarine and the wall of water was its bow wave.

It was being escorted by a flotilla of police motor-launches, rising and plunging into the submarine's wash like tiny ducklings struggling to keep up with their mother. The wall of water had almost reached me and, flinging the helm hard over, I was racing back to the safety of the fairway buoy at full throttle when one of the 'ducklings' broke away from the flotilla and hurtled alongside Halcyon in a flurry of spray. 'You are not a good target on our radar,' bellowed an angry, uniformed gent from the wheelhouse door. 'You must get out of the channel at once; you are in considerable danger. There are three large warships astern of us. Please wait until they are safely past, then you may proceed.'

Before I could enquire how long I would have to wait, the wheelhouse door was slammed shut and, with a roar of engines, the launch shot away, leaving *Halcyon* rolling and pitching in its wake and sending mugs and pans in the galley crashing to the floor. Steering *Halcyon* back to the fairway buoy I was shaking with the realisation of the near miss with the submarine. It was one of the hazards of sailing in the vicinity of shipping lanes, but a nerve-wracking start to my cruise.

I had sailed from Fairlie on the lower Clyde that morning in *Halcyon*, my 9.75 metre gaff-rigged Keyhaven Yawl, heading for Loch Ranza on the Isle of Arran to pick up a friend, Pip Siddle. He was to come with me round the notorious Mull of Kintyre on the first leg of what I had planned would be a lengthy cruise to the Outer Hebrides and the remote islands of St Kilda, and it seemed as if the weather gods were conspiring with Her Majesty's Navy to keep me stranded between the islands of Bute and Great Cumbrae. Fuming and swearing had little effect! The swirling mists continued to swirl, and well over an hour went by before the three sombre Navy ships slid silently by and followed the submarine into the gloom.

Although April had just given way to May there was an icy chill in the air and, eager to be on my way, I shoved the engine into gear again, hoping that my masthead radar reflector was flashing like a beacon on the radar set of any ship still invisible in the mist. I gave the required blast on my pitifully inadequate foghorn to indicate a vessel under way, and nervously steered *Halcyon* across the half-mile-wide buoyed channel, bounced through the tide rip off the southern tip of the Isle of Bute, and set a course for Arran. Visibility continued to be poor and later, when a position plot showed I had only five miles to run to the entrance of Kilbrannan Sound at the north end of Arran, I went below to put the kettle on the stove to make a mug of coffee.

I arrived back in the cockpit just as a blazing sun was dissolving the mist and revealing what appeared to be the entire Clyde fishing fleet scattered across the sea about a mile ahead of me. Wondering if I would ever reach Arran that day, and faced with having to make a long detour to avoid nets and trawl wires, I tetchily swung *Halcyon* onto a new course. Two hours went by before I eventually reached the Arran coast, following it until an ancient stone castle at the head of a bay came into view marking the entrance to the haven of Loch Ranza. With *Halcyon* securely attached to a visitors' mooring, I rowed ashore to a warm welcome from my friends the Siddles. Glass in hand, in their lovely house close to the water's edge, I was soon enjoying the hospitality of Pip and his wife Chris, which, true to the custom on Scottish islands, extended into the night.

The name of Dr Thomas Harrison Butler, the medical man who rattled the die-hards of sailing boat design in the 1920s with his radical theories on yacht stability, is almost as legendary in the world of wooden boats as Noah himself. The inventive doctor was famous for his ingenious 'metacentric shelf' analysis, a naval architect's term for a guide to achieving near-perfect stability in a boat; and his unique designs produced yachts noted for their easy handling. His far-reaching ideas made him world-famous, but it never affected his humility; and according to an old marine surveyor friend of mine who knew him, he would probably have enjoyed meeting John Jago, a Yorkshire lad who was one of his most ardent fans. John was destined to be a doctor, but he had a secret ambition to be a boatbuilder and dared not reveal it.

Pressured into following his father into medicine, John knew that if he had mentioned one morning over the breakfast cornflakes that he would have preferred to trade his stethoscope and scalpels for an adze and a box of wood-chisels and become a boatbuilder instead of a doctor, the family reaction would have triggered off earthquake detectors around the world. So he knuckled down, passed his medical exams, and ended up with a wife and family and a partnership in a medical practice in Seascale, on the Cumbrian coast.

Unlike his hero Dr Harrison Butler, who had a flair for designing boats, Dr John Jago had a natural gift for building them, and his attention to detail and brilliant workmanship resulted in some exceptionally fine boats being built in his very limited spare time. But he had to wait until near retirement before he had the time to start building what he called his 'dream ship'. The difficulty of obtaining quality hardwood where he lived forced him to drop his plan to build a 9.75 metre Harrison Butler cutter with a carvel hull and, impressed with the designs of the celebrated naval architect Jack Laurent Giles, he decided to build the little-known Keyhaven Yawl, an attractive single-chine yacht, planked with marine plywood and coated with epoxy resin inside and out.

It had an overall length of 9.75 metres without the bowsprit, the beam a touch under 3.35 metres and a draft of plate up, 1 metre and plate down, 2 metres; the unusual sail plan had a flying jib, boomed staysail, gaff-rigged main and a stand-ing lug mizzen. Working entirely alone he built the hull, cut the keelson out of a huge oak log with only a handsaw, laminated the awkward curved transom and constructed a superb 11 metre spruce main mast with a lovely taper, and a 6 metre mizzen mast to match it. Several years were to go by before the last screw was driven home, the last dab of varnish applied, and John was able to transport his 'dream ship', named *Halcyon* – meaning calm, peaceful, happy – thirty miles up the Cumbrian coast and launch it into the grimy waters of Maryport marina. But it was a dream that was to turn horribly sour.

He had only managed two short trips across the Irish Sea to the Isle of Man when he was taken seriously ill, and told his sailing days were over. All the years of dedicated hard slog, the pain, the sweat and the dream, were to no avail. Heart-broken, he left *Halcyon* for sale in Maryport marina, and there she lay for over two years, deteriorating rapidly.

I came across her quite by chance when I transported a 26-foot classic wooden boat I had restored down to Maryport from the Clyde to be sold, and I was instantly drawn to the strongly built, though horribly neglected, wooden yawl which was tied up in the marina and had for me the appealing 'I'd like to belong to you' look of a puppy in a pet shop.

'It would be ideal for a wooden boat fanatic like you,' laughed the manager when I went to the marina office and he handed me *Halcyon*'s keys. 'There hasn't been a single offer for it since it was tied up two years ago.'

Walking round the spacious deck and looking at the spars, the ground tackle and the beautifully made varnished mahogany skylight, I felt a tremendous thrill of excitement and recalled the words of Alan Villiers when he found the *Joseph Conrad*: 'She was no ordinary ship.' When I opened the companionway doors, one whiff of the musty wooden smell from below was all I needed. I was in love!

By an odd coincidence John Jago had been my family's GP when I lived in Cumbria, and it eased the anguish of parting with *Halcyon* when he found out who wanted to buy her. Events moved fast. With a clean bill of health from a marine surveyor, and some financial help from a friend, within the week my name appeared on the ship's register as the new owner. It wasn't the only time in my life I had fallen in love with a lady at first sight, then when I looked closer wondered what had attracted me; and seen from any angle, *Halcyon* was a mess. A large percentage of the woodwork, including both masts, had originally been varnished, but two years of exposure to the elements had lifted the varnish off, and the whole boat above water level was streaked with a green slime.

Most worrying of all was the 28 hp Volvo engine. It was seized solid, but by a stroke of luck Keith Hindle, the owner of a boat moored close to *Halcyon*, turned out to be a diesel engineer. Having removed the cylinder head and managed to free the pistons, he fitted the whole lot back together with new gaskets from a box of engine spares I found on board, and when he pressed the starter button the engine burst into life and ran beautifully.

It took several weeks of hard work before *Halcyon* was ready for the journey to my home port on the Clyde; but finally, on a calm starry night, accompanied by the friend who helped me to buy *Halcyon*, I motored out of Maryport into the lumpy Irish Sea. After a two-day passage by way of the Mull of Galloway and the North Channel, we reached Fairlie on the Clyde where I had a mooring.

Dr John Jago died some time later, but on the day we finalised the sale and shook hands he told me he loved sailing in Scotland but had never been to the Outer Hebrides. 'If you ever sail *Halcyon* to the Hebrides, take me with you; I've always wanted to sail to Saint Kilda,' he laughed.

I promised I would, and even though he could only have been with me in spirit when, on a foggy morning in May, I cast off from Fairlie and sailed for Loch Ranza on my way to the Hebrides, I had a feeling he was aboard and keeping a watchful eye on his 'dream ship'.

2

SCOTLAND'S CAPE HORN – GOD'S ISLAND

Lulled into a deep sleep by the combination of a strenuous day, a large dinner and several glasses of a fine malt whisky, I woke with a start the next morning and jumped out of bed at the Siddles, convinced I had overslept and would not be off the headland of the Mull of Kintyre when the tide turned; but when I checked my watch it was only 7 a.m. and there was no need for panic – we had plenty of time. It was a beautiful, calm morning with not a sign of the troublesome mist, and through the bedroom window I could see *Halcyon* lying motionless on the mooring, red sails neatly furled and her varnished topsides caught in a solitary shaft of light from the sun rising over the mountain tops and shimmering like gold.

I followed a mouth-watering aroma of bacon and fresh coffee drifting up from the kitchen, and when we were all seated round the table it was obvious that Chris's philosophy was that no sailor should put to sea without a good breakfast. Sausages, fried eggs, rich Stornoway black pudding, Scotch white pudding, tomatoes and mushrooms had joined the bacon, and to make sure that no one left the table hungry, a stack of toast, butter, marmalade and jam and a cafetière of coffee as big as a bucket followed it. Unable to move until the breakfast invasion had levelled out in my stomach, I took the opportunity to get the charts out and study our route plan.

Pip was to sail with me round the Mull of Kintyre, jokingly – and sometimes not so jokingly – known as Scotland's Cape Horn, but had to return home when we reached the island of Gigha (Gee-a) – God's Island, to take Chris on holiday. Ironically it was only fourteen nautical miles from Loch Ranza in a straight line,

*Pip Siddle approaching
the Mull of Kintyre*

albeit on the west side of the Kintyre Peninsula, but sixty by sea. Many pilot books seemed to make the timing of the turn of the tide for rounding the Mull into a mathematical problem based on the tide tables of the Clyde, but a retired sea captain friend of mine had a simple solution.

'If you're going west, be off the headland of the Mull at High Water Belfast.'

According to Reeds Nautical Almanac, High Water Belfast that day was at 4 p.m., and the distance to the Mull from Loch Ranza about thirty-five nautical miles, so, leaving at 9 a.m. and maintaining five knots over the ground, I reckoned we should arrive bang on time. Pip grunted his approval and, while he busied himself making sure he had essential stores like his pipe and tobacco, Chris organised a sea bag with his spare clothes and oilies. With half an hour to go to our leaving time, Chris helped us to carry the inflatable down a concrete slip by the house, where we were confronted with a major problem.

Pip was built like a mast of the *Cutty Sark*, and often seemed as tall, but his metacentric shelf was somewhere around his ankles, which made him prone to capsizing; and the time he was most likely to go keel over masthead was when he stepped into a dinghy, going to or from a boat. I pulled the inflatable as tightly as I could against the slip and, aware of an imminent calamity, Chris clung on to her pipe-puffing gargantuan and persuaded him to slide onto the seat rather than stand on it. By this means I managed to transport him out to *Halcyon*, and with superhuman effort transfer him from the dinghy to the boarding ladder and onto the deck. The dinghy was deflated and stowed, and when the engine had warmed up I gave Pip a shout to slip the mooring and, with a barely audible grunt on the foghorn to Chris waving from the shore, we were on our way.

Sailing up or down Kilbrannan Sound, the corridor of water that separates the Isle of Arran from the Kintyre Peninsula, is often an exercise in avoiding the fleet of trawlers that fish from the Kintyre port of Carradale, but when we cleared Loch Ranza we had the Sound to ourselves. By 1 p.m. the distinctive hump of Davaar Island at the entrance to Campbeltown Loch, well-known for its unusual religious cave paintings until mindless vandals painted over them, was abeam to starboard. Boat owners Pip had previously crewed for had assured me he was very useful in an emergency; and though with the perfect conditions we were enjoying he had not been put to the test, his massive bulk was very useful for blocking off a cool northerly breeze that sprang up just as I went below to put the kettle on. When I emerged into the cockpit with mugs of tea and sandwiches, I was surprised to discover he had also sheltered me from a shower of rain. The rain had gone, but a bank of cloud drifting down from the north had devoured the sun and the temperature had plummeted noticeably; but, snug in our oilies, we wedged ourselves in the cockpit as *Halcyon* rolled past the notorious Paterson's Rock and approached the black cliffs of Sanda Island.

Noted for its eccentric owners, for having one of the most isolated pubs in the UK, and for adventurous Irishmen who regularly braved the hazardous twenty-mile crossing from Northern Ireland in fast inflatable boats for a Sunday pint, Sanda was also the milestone that marked the end of the eastern side of the Kintyre Peninsula and the turning point for the Mull. I had just set the autopilot on a course a touch north of west that would keep us two miles offshore to avoid a nasty tide race that curves round the headland, when a Royal Navy patrol ship, bristling with guns and looking very businesslike, appeared as if from nowhere. It charged towards us at about twenty knots, displaying a healthy disregard for the price of marine diesel, but though we waved as it shot by, the only reply we got was a massive wash that flung *Halcyon* into a trough, and might have resulted in a major incident, with a court martial for the captain, had not Pip managed to stop his beloved pipe from going over the side.

There are legions of horror stories told about yacht passages round the Mull of Kintyre, and in wind against tide conditions I have experienced huge waves rearing from all directions threatening to overwhelm the boat. But in calm weather with a favourable tide it is no more menacing than a duck pond, and such were the conditions when at 4 p.m. the tide reached its height in Belfast Lough. Bucking convention, the ebb poured north instead of south, compressed between Northern Ireland and Scotland, until half an hour or so later it discharged like a fire hose at the gateway to the Atlantic Ocean and swept *Halcyon* round the Mull of Kintyre and past the lighthouse at eleven knots, and only five of those were contributed by the engine. On the west side of the peninsula, the ebb that had taken us round the Mull became the flood that helped us along the sixteen miles to Gigha, and at close on 8 p.m. *Halcyon* was swinging on a visitors' mooring in Ardminish Bay and we were relaxing in the cockpit, glasses of whisky to hand, with the Siddle pipe belching smoke like a transom-mounted barbecue.

Gigha is an island that, once you have reached you find so enchanting it is difficult to leave and, captivated by its spell, Pip decided to spend an extra day. BBC Radio Scotland's lady weather forecaster promised a hot sun, and we spent some time basking in it outside the Gigha Hotel, fending off the heat with pints of cool beer before enjoying a delightful walk that led us to Achamore House, once lived in by the Horlick family, of bedtime drink fame. Pip departed on MacBrayne's ferry for the mainland early next morning and I felt sad to see him go. He was one of the few people I would have felt comfortable sailing round the world with.

The realisation that I was now sailing alone was brought home to me in the afternoon, when the sun dived behind a black cloud and, within minutes, a fierce squall roared in from the east and churned the water of the anchorage into a mass of angry breakers. In good weather Ardminish Bay is paradise, but in a strong easterly wind it can be sheer hell, as that intrepid ocean sailor, Frank Mulville, discovered when his yacht *Iskra* was wrecked in Ardminish Bay in the 1990s, and he and his wife were rescued by helicopter. He survived to rebuild the boat and write a book about it, but with *Halcyon* leaping up and down like a wild horse I now had my own survival to think about. The only safe shelter was in West Tarbert Bay on the north-west side of Gigha, and it meant a five-mile trip in rough conditions; there was no time to lose and, letting go the mooring, I headed out into Gigha Sound.

The squalls were becoming more vicious with every blast, and even under bare poles *Halcyon* heeled over until her lee scuppers were under water. At the head of the Sound, I could see that the narrow gap between the northern tip of Gigha and the outlying island group of An Dubh-sgeir was white with breakers, but I knew it to be deep water and, sending *Halcyon* crashing through it, I steered for the shelter of Eilean Garbh, an island at the top extremity of West Tarbert Bay, joined to Gigha by a natural causeway. Cautiously sounding my way behind it, I dropped anchor in five metres and the contrast was surreal. It was flat calm, and with a sigh of relief I brewed a pot of tea and sat on deck in the sun, hardly able to believe that on a small island like Gigha there could be gale conditions on the east side and an almost tropical contrast on the west.

During the early evening, a smart ketch with its mizzen sail in tatters came scudding in and anchored a short distance from me; and when the crew rowed past heading for a leg stretch ashore, they said it had been blown out by a squall in Gigha Sound. In more enlightened days, before politicians reduced the Royal Yacht to a tourist attraction, I might have been joined by royalty; West Tarbert Bay was a favourite anchorage when the Queen was on a tour of west Scotland aboard

Britannia. The ship once steamed past me when I was in a small yacht that did not have an ensign, so I waved my souwester. To my astonishment, a seaman was despatched at the double and dutifully dipped the white ensign. It made my day.

I was forced to stay for two days while the easterly wind churned up the sea beyond the edge of the bay, but in my sun trap I was able to explore the shoreline and photograph the masses of wild flowers abundant on the west side of Gigha. On my wanderings I met a cheery crofter who was very knowledgeable about local history and, while we leant back against a gate, he told me that Gigha had been exploited by a succession of wealthy owners who only wanted the island as a glorified holiday home and were not interested in investing money in it. But now the future was looking a lot brighter. He said the tenants had managed to raise the money to buy Gigha as a community project and it had already attracted newcomers to build houses and live on the island.

Back on board, I spread the charts out on deck to plan my route to the Hebrides. The quickest and most direct route was through the Sound of Islay, a water highway with a fierce tide that ran between the islands of Islay and Jura. BBC Radio Scotland's lady forecaster said that the weather was settling down with a nice fat high-pressure system drifting over Scotland and we could look forward to a hot sunny spell, so I made ready to leave the following day. The disadvantages were that there would be no wind for sailing, and I would have to be off the entrance to the Sound at 8 a.m. to catch the turn of the tide. It was ten miles from Gigha and I set my alarm clock for 5 a.m.

3

NEPTUNE'S NAG – TINKER'S HOLE – LOCHBUIE'S CHALLENGE

A habit I have of leaving an alarm clock in the metal galley sink, so that when it goes off it amplifies the sound, has never been appreciated by people who have sailed with me; but it certainly leaves everyone in no doubt that it is time to get up and, when the awful racket shattered my sleep at 5 a.m., I felt sure there would be a barrage of nautical oaths from the ketch, but when I looked out it had gone. It had been flying the ensign of the Irish Republic and probably left during the night to take the tide south.

The morning was breathtakingly beautiful, with not a cloud in the sky or a ripple on the water and, while sipping a leisurely coffee in the dew-soaked cockpit, I shared my breakfast bacon sandwiches with a raft of cooing eider ducks and a pair of swans. I felt desperately sorry to be leaving such a tranquil anchorage but, once I had cleared the bay and broken the spell, I was glad to be on my way again and, as the new sun climbed higher and bathed Islay's coastline and Jura's three distinctive conical hills, known as the Paps, in a warm glow, the effect was dramatic.

The Sound of Islay has a tidal stream that does not allow for a sudden change of mind; once a boat with a small engine is committed to going north through the Sound it is too late to attempt to turn back. Below the lighthouse off McArthur's Head at the southern entrance to the Sound, it was as if *Halcyon* had been harnessed to one of Neptune's sea-horses which, having been prodded in the backside with his trident, took off like a demon, streaking past the ferry terminal of Port Askaig and the whisky distillery of Bunnahabhainn (Bunnahaven), until finally casting her loose abeam of Rubha a Mhail (Ruvaal), the most northerly tip of Islay. Helped along by five knots of Volvo power, Neptune's nag had whisked us through the ten miles of the Sound in exactly one hour. It took me longer than that to cover the next eight miles to the dubious refuge of Scalasaig pier on the island of Colonsay.

The sun was now a yellow orb in the sky and it was blisteringly hot; but, although boards had been fastened in place to protect yachts lying alongside the pier at Scalasaig, there was a slight but annoying swell that occasionally bashed *Halcyon* against them. It made life very uncomfortable while I was attempting to make sandwiches and coffee for lunch, and put me off the idea of staying the night. Every attempt I had ever made to stray beyond the pier, the hotel and the post office and get to know Colonsay had been burdened with problems, always because my visits to the island had been in small boats and there were no safe facilities catering for them.

Adjacent to the steamer pier was a fine sheltered harbour, but it was tidal and the island fathers had obviously not considered that dredging it and providing pontoons for visiting yachts could be a useful source of income. So, once more I got no further than the post office to send a card to a friend who was fanatical about the beauty of Colonsay, and I had promised to let her know if I visited the island. I was reluctant to leave when the weather was so exceptional, but Colonsay was not yacht-friendly, and only twelve miles away was the lovely island of Mull that had plenty of sheltered anchorages.

Pulling away from Scalasaig, I set a course that would take me to the Ross of Mull at the south-west corner of the island and the start of the passage through the infamous Torran Rocks to the Sound of Iona, and had covered only five miles or so when I was startled out of my wits by a minke whale leaping out of the water in front of *Halcyon* and landing with a tremendous crash that cascaded water over the deck and me. I knocked the engine into neutral to stop the propeller, and hardly had the first one submerged when another one jumped, then another, and I was so enthralled by the sight of the huge creatures leaping and playing like porpoises I completely forgot about my camera. By the time I had rushed below and grabbed it, they had completely disappeared and the sea was undisturbed for miles. It was an incredibly thrilling experience and I left my camera hanging round my neck just in case they appeared again, but they never did.

The first time I negotiated the intricate passage through the Torran Rocks (Thunderous Rocks), off the Ross of Mull, was in a ketch my wife and I were operating skippered charters with, and we had Mrs Thatcher's Attorney General and his family on board. It was pouring with rain, and with fog as thick as porridge visibility was about a metre. 'Are you sure you know where we are?' demanded her ladyship.

I should have told the truth and said, 'Madam, I haven't a clue, but I do know there are some dangerous submerged rocks on either side of us.' But I assured her all was well. Fortunately my navigation plots turned out to be accurate and we survived.

Making the passage between the rocks on a hot, sunny day was as easy as going along a canal and, creeping past the last of the submerged monsters that flashed its malevolent white teeth beneath the surface, I steered into the tiny anchorage of the Tinker's Hole, almost hidden between the island of Eilean Dubh and the island of Erraid, immortalised by Robert Louis Stevenson in his novel *Kidnapped*. I dropped anchor in the middle of the pool, gave the chain an extra bit of scope to allow for the strong tide and slid a lead angel down it for good measure. (An angel is a heavy weight designed to help the anchor grip the bottom.)

A large sloop had arrived ahead of me and the two occupants were in the throes of anchoring close in to Erraid and using a dinghy to take a stern warp to a ring on a rock. The chap in the dinghy had tied the warp round his waist to be able to drag it from the boat, but it was too short and he was still a couple of feet away from the ring when it ran out.

Determined to get there, he rowed furiously and with a supreme effort grabbed the ring with one hand but the warp from his waist to the boat was as tight as a fiddle string. 'Slack off the anchor chain,' he screamed, but in his hurry his mate must have pressed the wrong button on the electric anchor winch and, instead of slacking off, the chain started to come in with a run and the boat lurched forward. The man was being stretched as though he was on a medieval torture rack and with a shriek he let go of the ring, and the strain on the warp round his waist catapulted him out of the dinghy and landed him in the pool with an almighty splash. By now the anchor was above the surface and, caught by the tide, the boat began to drift rapidly past *Halcyon*, towing the man in the water behind it. Throwing a warp to the elderly gent on deck, I made the boat fast alongside, and eventually they sorted themselves out.

I launched my inflatable and retrieved their dinghy, and they motored away and anchored again, this time without the stern warp! A couple of hours later I was below preparing my evening meal when there was a rap on the hull, and when I looked out it was the man who had been in the water. He was the owner of the boat and he had brought me a bottle of whisky as a gesture of thanks.

In need of a leg stretch, the following morning I rowed across to Erraid (Arthraigh – tidal island) and clambered through knee-deep heather. When he lived on the island in the 1800s, Robert Louis Stevenson described it as 'the roughest kind of walking', and two hundred years later it was still very rough. Dripping with sweat, I struggled upwards, and the reward was a stupendous view from the island summit across to the Torran Rocks and beyond to Colonsay. Through my binoculars I could see the bleak stone towers of Dubh Artach lighthouse west of Colonsay, and Skerryvore south of the island of Tiree.

One of the dynasty of Scottish lighthouse builders, Robert Louis Stevenson stayed on Erraid when it was used as a base while Thomas Stevenson, his father, was building Dubh Artach, but lighthouse building was not for him. The stormy sea and the wild location of Erraid were the inspiration for his great novel *Kidnapped*, in which the hero, David Balfour, was shipwrecked on the Torran Rocks and marooned on the island. It was a strange feeling to stand on the same spot as RLS and imagine him staring out to sea and scribbling his inspirations into a notebook.

The old gents in the sloop had gone when I got back to *Halcyon*, and in the cockpit they had left me a parting gift of a plastic bag containing a loaf, a carton of milk, packets of sausages and bacon and six eggs. It was a generous gift that would save me searching out a shop in an area where they were few and far between. Stowing the inflatable and the anchor, I threaded *Halcyon* through a narrow rock-strewn channel into the Sound of Iona, where the 6th-century Irish monk Columba had founded the famous Abbey.

One story about the building of it tells how, in order to overcome a pagan influence, Columba buried alive his best friend Oran in the foundations. Suffering pangs of conscience he uncovered Oran's face a few days later, but when Oran spoke and said, 'Heaven is not as it has been written; neither is hell as commonly supposed,' Columba was appalled by what he considered was blasphemy, and promptly shovelled rocks over him again.

Not being a follower of any particular religion I am inclined to share Oran's view of the hereafter, but on the occasions when I have sat alone in the Abbey I have experienced an inexplicable peace. 'Whose piety would not grow warmer among the ruins of Iona?' observed the venerable Dr Johnson during his tour of the Scottish Highlands and Islands in 1773.

Millions of years ago, when the architects of Scotland's offshore land masses had finished pummelling Mull into shape, they had lots of pieces left over and very obligingly scattered them over the sea on the west side of the island. Invaders who settled permanently in the area gave them intriguing names like Lunga, Fladda, Staffa, Eorsa, Inch Kenneth, Samalan, Ulva and Gometra; and later, when travel became fashionable with the gentry, composers like Mendelssohn wrote music in their honour. His 'Fingal's Cave' overture captures perfectly a musical picture of the dark, brooding, storm-lashed island of Staffa, with its massive high-roofed cave foaming with surf. I had sailed by Staffa many times but had never actually put foot on the island, and I hoped that this time the flat-calm conditions would enable me to land; but I should have known better. The perfect conditions had brought every tripper boat for miles, and they were coming and going at the rocky landing like wasps to a jam pot.

Fortunately, only a few miles to the west of Staffa there was a string of islands where few tripper boats ever ventured. Floating on the glistening sea like a necklace of jewels were the mystical Treshnish Islands; once inhabited, but now empty and silent save for the plaintive cries of colonies of seabirds. I steered for the southern and most distinctive of the group, Bac Mor, better known to fishermen as the Dutchman's Cap; seen from a certain angle it resembles a conical cap with two side wings. The noise from the nesting seabirds was deafening and, had I had a crew with me to handle *Halcyon*, I might have been able to land and photograph them; but I dared not risk it on my own and turned north to look at Lunga and Fladda.

They were so small, and so lacking in land which could be cultivated that I wondered how anyone could have survived on either of them, but on Cairn na Burgh Mor, the most northerly of the group, there were the ruins of a castle once owned by the MacLeans of Duart Castle on Mull.

Legend has it that during one of the many on-going disputes with their neighbours, the MacLeans of Lochbuie, they captured the clan chief and imprisoned him in the island castle. Convinced he would never be desperate enough to produce an heir with her, they marooned him with the ugliest woman on Mull as a servant. Perhaps fortified by the sea air and a wholesome diet of seabirds' eggs, Lochbuie rose to the challenge – though whether he waited until it was pitch dark in the servant's quarters or just closed his eyes and got on with it, history does not record. In the fullness of time the facially disadvantaged lady presented him with a son and heir, and somehow mother and child escaped to Mull where, years later, the son is said to have won back his father's land at Lochbuie.

Leaving Cairn na Burgh Mor I was faced with a choice. Should I go into the delightful little anchorage of Acairseid Mhor, a shallow pool on the north end of the Isle of Gometra, which was only three miles to the east but was completely wild and isolated; or make for Arinagour, eight miles away on the island of Coll which, with a hotel, a church, a shop that sold marine diesel and a ferry connection to Oban, had the status of the island capital? It also had a few visitors' moorings. Of the two I would have preferred the solitude of Acairseid Mhor, but there was still a lot of the day left and, reluctant to squander such rare weather, I plumped for a third option, to head for the lovely island of Canna. It meant a thirty-mile slog under engine, but I had plenty of diesel and Canna was ideally placed for hopping across to Barra, at the southern end of the Outer Hebrides.

Decision made, I lashed a light tarpaulin over the boom to give me some protection from the blazing sun – the first time I had ever done that in Scotland – filled a flask with hot water to make tea, and set a course that would clear the Cairns of Coll, a group of rocks at the northerly tip of the island. After stopping briefly, and unsuccessfully, to try to photograph a couple of uncooperative basking sharks, I was on my way. A light easterly breeze sprang up as I neared the Cairns of Coll and, excited at the prospect of a run to Canna under sail, I rushed to untie the spinnaker pole ready to boom the jib out. Alas, the wind gods were just taunting me! The breeze died as quickly as it had arrived and, as if to ram home the superiority of engine power, MacBrayne's Outer Isles car ferry *Lord of the Isles* appeared at speed from the direction of the Sound of Mull and surged smugly by on its way to Barra, leaving me bouncing in its wake.

Many a poet and writer has struggled to find a superlative worthy enough to describe the beauty of the panorama of the Small Isles, spread across the sea to the north of Coll, and while *Halcyon* ploughed a steady furrow through the unusually placid Sea of the Hebrides I tried to capture them on my camera. Tiny low-lying Muck (the isle of pigs), Eigg (a notch) with its huge Sgurr of rock dominating the skyline like the bow of a ship, the romantic and mystical Island of Rum (isle of the ridge) bristling with sharp pointed mountain tops and, my favourite, Canna (porpoise island), long, green, and flat-topped, tucked against the island of Sanday. Between them is formed one of the most sheltered natural harbours in the west of Scotland and, despite its lack of facilities, it is a popular anchorage for cruising yachts and an overnight resting place for the crews of fishing boats.

The crew of a becalmed yacht rising and falling in the swell half a mile from Canna declined my offer of a tow in and, giving a treacherous rock in the harbour entrance a wide berth, I steered *Halcyon* past the old stone pier and dropped anchor astern of a lovely old ketch flying the Norwegian flag.

It was early evening but still remarkably warm and, feeling horribly dehydrated, I was in need of a cold beer. Unlike Sir Francis Chichester in *Gypsy Moth*, I had no brewery-owning pal to build me a keg into the bilge of my boat to keep beer cool, but I had the next best thing. I had towed two cans of lager alongside *Halcyon* in a bag made from a piece of fishing net, and they were like nectar. Too hot to face a cooked meal, I managed a small carton of yoghurt and turned into my bunk.

It was when crewing on fishing boats as a boy that I first visited Canna and grew very fond of it. At that time, the island was owned by John Lorne Campbell who, with the writer Sir Compton Mackenzie of *Whisky Galore* fame, worked hard to improve the working conditions of fishermen and had something of a hero status. But since then, the National Trust for Scotland had acquired Canna and I was worried that they would spoil it. For all its gentlemanly facade, the Trust was as money-hungry as any private commercial enterprise, and I had visions of boatloads of tourists arriving to buy maps at the inevitable Ranger-staffed Visitor Centre, before tramping off on way-marked 'adventure' trails.

Fearing the worst, I rowed ashore the following morning to look round the island settlement, but nothing appeared to have changed; and the only complaint a local I chatted to by the island post office had about the National Trust for Scotland was their plan to 'import' new residents to the island who, he predicted, would be clamouring to get back to the mainland once they had experienced their first winter of island life.

The BBC had promised another brilliant day and I walked up Compass Hill, a viewpoint above the harbour, which once had an evil reputation for being magnetic and affecting the compasses of sailing ships, often with fatal consequences. The man at the post office told me that rats from the wrecks of ships had overrun Canna and wiped out the seabird colonies, but the Trust had almost eradicated the pests and birds were nesting again.

Back at the harbour, I did my own bit for wildlife conservation when I came across a black-backed gull completely entangled in a discarded fishing line and with the barbed hook through its beak. The terrified bird put up a fierce fight, but I managed to hold it long enough to get rid of the hook and unwind the line; though, just as I was about to launch it into the air, it rather ungratefully jabbed its vicious beak into my thumb.

Putting it down to an over-zealous expression of thanks, I covered the wound with a plaster to stop the flow of blood and wandered round the harbour and over a bridge to the lesser-known island of Sanday, where an old Scottish Presbyterian chapel and an even older Catholic Church stood in defiant opposition, though their combined congregations would barely have filled a pew. The buildings were both austere and empty, but the Catholic Church had a plaque dedicated to the former owner of Canna, John Lorne Campbell, and his wife Margaret Fay Shaw, a talented American lady who, after her husband died in the 1980s, continued to live on Canna until her death in 2004 at the age of 101.

Fishermen paint the names of their boats on a rock at Canna harbour

When I motored *Halcyon* out of Canna harbour after breakfast the next day and pointed the bow in the direction of Barra, thirty miles away, the surface of the Sea of the Hebrides was so still it was like a vast expanse of dark blue glass. It was eerie. Even the Admiralty Pilot warns that the bottom of the Sea of the Hebrides is very uneven; steep seas may be encountered and it is twice as rough as the Minch. As a result it has an unsavoury reputation, and there are plenty of stories told about wild journeys from Oban to Barra on the car ferry.

One of MacBrayne's captains gleefully used to tell a story about a maintenance engineer based in Oban who had to visit the Hebrides at regular intervals. He was so terrified of the sea he used to get very drunk before the ship sailed, then sleep it off in his bunk – in those days MacBrayne's ships provided passenger cabins. One day, well fortified with whisky as usual before sailing, he fell into his bunk on the ship and when he sobered up several hours later was relieved to see the ship moored to a quay.

'That was the quietest run I've ever had to Barra,' he said to the steward who brought him a mug of tea. 'I hardly felt the boat move.'

The steward gave him an odd look and replied, 'We haven't left Oban yet, sir. There was a severe gale warning and we didn't sail. The sea is still very rough but the captain says he'll go for it. We're leaving in ten minutes!'

With enormous sea eagles reported to have nested on Canna, I hoped I would see one during the long trip to Barra, or at least a minke whale, a basking shark or a school of porpoises, but the oppressive heat seemed to have made all the wildlife completely lethargic and there was not even a humble herring-gull floating on the water. I tried trolling a line in the hope of catching a fish for tea, but after an hour without as much as a nibble I reeled the line in and changed the evening menu to tuna pasta. A purple haze on the horizon made it difficult to make out the island of Barra, but when I was about ten miles off I could see the summit of Heaval, 382 metres, the island's highest hill, poking above the haze and lit by the sun.

It was a handy mark to steer on and, just under seven hours after leaving Canna, I motored past the remarkable sight of a full-rigged ship, under canvas, lying motionless on the sea. Then, ticking off the fairway buoys on the chart, I slipped past the forbidding ramparts of Kisimul Castle, the stronghold of the ancient Clan MacNeil, built on an isolated rock. From there it was just a short hop to the ferry terminal and the luxury of a visitors' mooring.

I had arrived on one of an archipelago of over five hundred islands, known to the Vikings as Hav-bred-ey – 'Isles on the Edge of the Sea'; what geologists fondly refer to as 'the oldest chunks of rock in Europe'; Tourist Boards romantically call 'the Western Isles'; were known to the Gaels as Innis nan Cat – 'The Long Island'; and map-makers insist are the Outer Hebrides.

4

BARRA – THE WICKED PRINCESS – ARCHIE SEES THE LIGHT

Geographically, a south-to-north cruise through the Hebrides should start about twelve miles south of Barra at Berneray, the southernmost island of the group, on which stands Barra Head lighthouse, winking a welcome and a warning across the grey Atlantic. It would then take in Mingulay, associated with the Mingulay Boat Song, written by Hugh Robertson, the conductor of the famed Glasgow Orpheus Choir, and performed by choirs the world over, though it is said it was never sung on the island.

The Mingulay islanders had a rather unique way of keeping the population topped up. If a man's wife died, he could appeal to the laird, MacNeil of Barra, to provide him with a replacement. On a visit to Mingulay in 1695 Martin Martin reported, 'The woman's name being told him, he immediately goes to her, carrying with him a bottle of strong water for their entertainment at the marriage, which is then consummated.' Widows could also claim a similar perk.

Pabbay, the next island in the chain, was inhabited for many years; but when every man on the island was tragically lost in a storm in 1897 while out fishing, the population never recovered, and it is now the haunt of sheep and seabirds. Nearby Sandray was reputed to be inhabited by fairies, but nowadays they are more likely to be outnumbered by archaeologists excavating the island's many Neolithic settlements. Having few places on which to land and no safe haven for boats, all these small islands are now rarely visited, which is probably just as well. Were they still inhabited, the local Tourist Board would have a hard time trying to promote 'Bed and Breakfast Accommodation' where the locals had a rule that, if male and female strangers visited the islands, they were not allowed to sleep together even if they were married.

The picturesque island of Vatersay, with its achingly beautiful white sandy beaches, is the last in this minor group, once known as the Bishop's Islands, and has the good fortune to lie close to Barra and be separated only by a narrow sound. The crofters used to swim their cattle across Vatersay Sound en route to Oban market via MacBrayne's ferry; but in the 1990s a prize bull was drowned, and government ministers had their arms twisted to meet the cost of joining Vatersay to Barra with a concrete causeway.

Legends abound about the origin of the name Barra, and one popular story tells how a 6th-century Irish missionary named Barr was sent to fill a post on a Hebridean island because the natives had eaten his predecessor. Perhaps in recognition of his ability to avoid ending up as the main ingredient of a communal haggis, the island was eventually called Barr's island which, when the Vikings arrived on the scene, they knew as Barr-oy and today everyone knows as Barra. A man from Barra I worked with on fishing boats used to joke that the island was shaped like the aerial view of a turtle with its neck and head facing north forming a promontory, and it represented the speed of life on the island.

Like so many Hebridean harbour towns, Castlebay on Barra had been a major fish-landing port and curing centre during the height of the herring fishing boom in the 19th century, but when herring stocks began to decline, so did Castlebay. Deserted fish-curing stations fell into ruin, and the rest of the town might have gone the same way had it not been for the new saviour, tourism. It was given a tremendous boost by the hilarious film made on Barra of Sir Compton Mackenzie's classic story of Hebridean life, *Whisky Galore*. Castlebay's steep main street, running down to the harbour, featured prominently in the film and it aroused worldwide interest in the relatively little-known island.

A very enthusiastic and helpful man in charge of the island's heritage centre told me proudly that Barra had become renowned as a centre for the promotion of Celtic music and the Gaelic language, and he told me an intriguing legend about how a ruthless princess won her man.

On Barra there once lived a band of fourteen heroes called the Feinn, and their chief was Fionn. Of Viking descent, they all had golden hair and blue eyes, and each was armed with a two-handed sword buckled round his waist, a shield carried on his left forearm and a dirk pushed into the top of his right stocking. They were a tough bunch and before a man could join the Feinns he had to survive an initiation test, where he had to prove he was an expert swordsman and was so strong he could hold his broadsword between the tip of his thumb and forefinger and hold it out at arm's length without a tremor. He had to jump over a tree as high as his forehead, creep under a tree no higher than his knee without shaking the leaves, stand so lightly on a rotten branch it did not break and, the biggest test of all, pull a thorn out of his foot while running at full speed.

Fionn, the chief, was rather sweet on the beautiful daughter of King Dubhan of Ireland and, hoping to persuade the king to grant him her hand in marriage, Fionn set out from Barra in a boat with his fourteen Feinns and sailed to Ireland. They were well received and wined and dined in splendour, though the king made it clear that Fionn was not high enough up the social ladder to marry a princess, and flatly refused to consider his request.

But the princess had fallen for the handsome blond from Barra, and the following morning asked her father to launch the royal galley so they could take Fionn and his men on a sea trip to admire the cliffs and the seabirds. 'But there's only room for sixteen people,' protested the king, 'and when you and myself and our own fourteen trusted followers are on board it would be risky to take Fionn and his followers as well.'

'Nonsense!' replied the princess. 'The sea is calm and there is room for all of us.'

So Fionn and his fourteen men scrambled on board, and off they sailed. But dark clouds began to fill the sky, and within minutes a strong wind had built up waves that threatened to swamp the overloaded galley. 'We must lighten the ship, O King,' cried the navigator, nicknamed Horse, 'and some must be thrown overboard.'

Not wishing to lose any of his dark-haired warriors, or upset the rules of hospitality by heaving Fionn and his fair-haired friends over the side, the king refused. But when his men insisted that some must go, he turned to the princess and said, 'You got us into this mess, you choose who should be thrown over the side.'

'All right,' replied the princess, 'but first I'll alter the seating arrangements.' She sat on the middle thwart, facing the stern and said, 'On my right in the stern let there be four followers of Fionn, most beautiful and glorious. Next to them I place five dark-haired warriors from the palace of my father, King of Ireland. As she spoke the men took their places. 'Now, two followers of Fionn, the son of Cumhail, and one dark-haired warrior – he that is called Horse. In the bow, three followers of Fionn, the stalwart and lovely one.'

They shunted round until nine of Fionn's and six of her father's men were now in line along the port side of the galley, and the princess continued. 'In the starboard bow I place one of my father's men, and next to him Fionn. The brave Fionn would not stand there unless I placed two dark-haired warriors beside him on his left. Then let two fair stalwarts from the palace of Fionn take their places. You my father, King of Ireland, shall stand amidships, with a trusted dark-haired warrior on either side of you. Now I place a follower of Fionn. Let two dark-haired giants stand beside him, then two of Fionn's men. Next to them let the last of the King's warriors take his place. And now, my father,' said the princess to the king, 'you shall count, beginning where I began, and every ninth man shall be thrown overboard.'

Confident that his clever daughter had organised it in such a way that he and his men would be saved, the king began to count from the first of the men in the stern on the port side, and was alarmed when every ninth man turned out to be one of his own warriors. Fifteen times he made the count then he himself was thrown into the sea.

Having won the man she wanted by craftily disposing of her father and his warriors, the merciless princess ordered the Feinns to sail to Barra, where Fionn married his dark-haired beauty, and probably lived in fear of his life ever after.

By an odd coincidence, I was browsing round a charity bookshop when I returned home after my Hebridean cruise and I discovered a copy of a book called *Hebridean Journey*, by Halliday Sutherland, in which he also related the legend and illustrated it with a sketch. I have reproduced Sutherland's plan of the galley showing how the princess arranged the men. The large white circle is Fionn and the small white circles are his men. The large black circle is where the King of Ireland stood, and the small black circles are his dark-haired warriors.

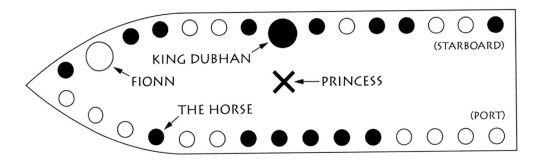

The man in the heritage centre said that for centuries the children of Barra used to play a game, using cockleshells for Fionn and his followers and mussel shells for the King of Ireland and his dark-haired warriors; but now that traditional games are no longer considered 'cool', the island youngsters will long have abandoned Fionn and probably have shifted their hero-worship to a gun-toting zombie on a computer playstation.

Having exhausted all of the town's attractions, I bought a book about the history of Kisimul Castle from the Tourist Information Centre and, leaving Castlebay shimmering in a stifling heat, rowed back to *Halcyon* laden with groceries, cartons of long-life milk, kippers and new potatoes for my tea, and a pack of cans of lager to restock the 'fridge'. It was too hot to do anything but laze and, sheltered from the sun under the tarpaulin over the boom, and comfortable on a bunk mattress with a can of lager to hand, I absorbed myself in the turbulent history of the Clan MacNeil.

Compared to some of the massive fortresses scattered around England, the castles of many of the Scottish clan chiefs are tiny; Dr Johnson on his tour of the Hebrides scornfully commented that, from the stones of one great medieval castle in England or Wales, all the castles he ever saw in Scotland could have been built. They might have been small, but the fortified homes of the clan chiefs were often set in the most romantic locations imaginable, and from Kisimul in Castle Bay the MacNeil chiefs ruled supreme.

They believed themselves superior to everyone, and every night a trumpeter appeared on the battlements of the castle, sounded a fanfare and proclaimed, 'Hear, O ye people, and listen, O ye nations. The great MacNeil of Barra having finished his meal, the princes of the earth may dine.'

The ceremony may have boosted the ego of the chief, but did little to impress Queen Elizabeth I of England, who was furious when the MacNeils plundered one of her ships in the Irish Sea and ordered James VI of Scotland to capture the clan chief Rory MacNeil and take him to Edinburgh for trial. The death penalty was inevitable, and before passing sentence James casually asked MacNeil why he had been foolish enough to attack one of Elizabeth's ships. It was a chance the wily Rory had been waiting for. 'I felt justified,' he said, 'in attacking the ships of the queen who had beheaded Your Majesty's mother.' There was no answer to that. James's mother was Mary, Queen of Scots and, hastily granting Rory a royal pardon, the king sent him on his way.

Though wild and violent, the MacNeils cared for their clansfolk. If one of the tenant's cows had twin calves or a sheep twin lambs, he would give one to the chief, but the arrangement worked out rather conveniently if the tenant's wife gave birth to twins. The chief was obliged to rear one of them with his own family and, visiting the islands in 1695, Martin Martin exclaimed, 'I have known one gentleman who had sixteen of these twins in his family at one time.' Another custom was an early form of dating agency where the chief found new wives for widowers and husbands for widows.

When the MacNeils ran short of funds in 1838 they had to sell Barra, and the islanders fell into the clutches of a tyrannical new owner, Colonel Gordon of Cluny, who terrorised the islanders when he declared that he was not receiving enough rent and, aided by the government, brought policemen to the island to destroy their houses, confiscate their stock and belongings, and drive the poor unfortunates off the island. Many were shipped penniless to America and Canada, and almost a century went by before a descendant of one of them, an American architect, Robert Lister MacNeil, became the 45th Chief of the Clan and bought back a large part of Barra, restoring Kisimul Castle as a clan heritage centre.

When I let go the mooring after breakfast, Kisimul Castle was bathed in the light of the morning sun and looked magnificent; and passing close to its ancient battlements I was reminded of an amusing incident involving Archie, one of the crew of a trawler I worked on in my youth.

He was what the islanders called 'a terrible man for the drink'. Ashore or aboard, he was seldom sober, and the skipper was heartily sick of him. We had put into Castlebay for a rest and to stock up on food, and the boat was barely tied up against the fish quay before Archie jumped ashore, headed for the nearest pub, and was well under the influence of the island brew when the locals tricked him into believing that Kisimul Castle was a pub that served free beer to fishermen.

Never one to miss a free drink, Archie 'borrowed' a rowing boat drawn up on the beach and set off for the island, but he was so drunk he forgot to tie the boat up and it drifted away, leaving him stranded. When he failed to show up the following morning it was the chance the skipper had been waiting for, and we put to sea without him. As we passed close to the castle, there was Archie shouting and waving to attract our attention. 'Let me aboard, Skipper,' he pleaded. 'I've seen the light and I've given up the drinking.'

'Och, well, I'm very pleased to be hearing it, Archie,' shouted the skipper. 'But the only light you'll be seeing on this ship is the stern light.' Pushing the engine control forward, he steered the boat out of the bay at full speed. We never saw Archie again, and, looking across to the rocks at the foot of the castle as *Halcyon* went by, I wondered if one of them might have been his petrified body!

Rounding the south cardinal buoy marking the entrance to Castle Bay, I set a course for the island of Eriskay, ten miles to the north.

5

WHISKY GALORE – LOCH EYNORT – SCOTLAND'S HEROINE

Barra had basked in glory when *Whisky Galore* was filmed in Castlebay, but it was actually in the Sound of Eriskay that, on 5 February 1941, the SS *Politician*, loaded with a mixed cargo which included over 260,000 bottles of whisky bound for the United States, struck a rock and was wedged on it for several hours before it slid into deep water. It was a heaven-sent gift to the islanders, who were suffering the severe restrictions of the war, and an Eriskay man living in Oban once told me that even hens, cattle and ponies staggered about drunk through picking at the whisky-soaked grass on the shore. He and his school pals had a hilarious time gathering up hundreds of tubes of toothpaste and having pitched battles squirting them at each other.

What the film which was made about it did not reveal was that a number of islanders ended up in gaol for illegal possession, but that would have spoiled the story. I had been told that the wreck of the ship could sometimes be seen, and I was hoping to photograph it.

If there is anywhere in the world to equal the beauty of Scotland's islands when the sky is clear, the sea calm, the visibility needle-sharp and the sun high in the sky, I have yet to see it; and the two-hour journey to Eriskay was sheer magic. The sea seemed to have come alive, with porpoises racing along at the sides of *Halcyon*, occasionally leaping into the air, and a magnificent display of minke whales ploughing through the water, heading south like a convoy of submarines. To starboard the sprawling bulk of Skye, mountainous Rum and rugged Canna seemed so close I felt I could have reached out and touched them, and the white sails of yachts and brightly coloured inshore fishing boats were everywhere.

The Gaelic word Acarsaid can be found on many charts of western Scotland and it means harbour – from Acair (to anchor). The name can also indicate a tricky entrance and Acarsaid Mhor – the big harbour on the south-east side of Eriskay – had leading beacons on the shore to mark a passage between two submerged rocks, and then a dog-leg channel between a starboard-hand buoy and perches that opened up into a large well-sheltered pool and the reward of visitors' moorings. The disadvantage of Acarsaid Mhor was the mile and a half that separated it from the shop, post office and the Sound at the opposite end of the island where the SS *Politician* sank, but the safe and snug anchorage more than compensated for it.

Acarsaid Mhor, Eriskay

The day was still young and, with a flask and sandwiches, camera and binoculars in my rucksack, I rowed over to a line of landing steps only to find it was low tide, the rocks were covered with a thick carpet of slippery kelp, and the bottom concrete step was so high above the low-water mark I could not lift the dinghy on to it.

Seeing me struggling, a fisherman who had been mending a net helped me to carry the dinghy up to the stone quay, and solved the mystery of the weird steps by laughingly explaining that the contractors who built the steps were not familiar with the sea, and had not allowed for the full fall of the tide.

The three-mile-long island of Eriskay is bleak, some say drab and featureless, but the islanders have introduced a splash of colour by painting the roofs of their houses in bright reds and greens, and the effect is most attractive. As I strode along the island's only road, with grass verges ablaze with wild flowers, it was clear from the many modern houses along the way that the local people no longer endured the survival existence of their forefathers when, in the 19th century, Eriskay was considered too poor even for sheep to survive. Arguably one of the most poignant of Gaelic love songs has its origin on Eriskay and, like the Mingulay Boat Song, is a great favourite with singers and choirs all over the world. It would have been more passionately expressed in Gaelic when the anonymous love-sick fisher-lad opened his heart with:

In the morning when I go
To the white and shining sea,
In the calling of the seals
Thy soft calling to me.

I could hear the tune and the words in my head and, hoping that my croaky voice would not startle the sheep, I broke into the chorus as I strode along:

Bheir me o, horo van o
Bheir me o, horo van ee
Bheir me o, o horo ho
Sad am I, without thee.

The Eriskay Love Lilt may have helped to publicise the little-known island but, to sympathisers of the Jacobite cause, Eriskay will forever be revered as the place where Prince Charles Edward Stuart, Bonnie Prince Charlie, landed for the first time in Scotland on 23 July 1745, from the French ship *Du Teillay* at the start of his ill-fated campaign to regain the British throne for the House of Stuart. Fleeing for his life after the catastrophe of the Battle of Culloden, he was later to be thankful again for the loyalty of the Hebrideans, who ignored the temptation of a massive ransom for his capture and helped him to escape.

In the tea bar of the community centre at Haun, the island's main settlement, there was a fine photograph of the SS *Politician*, but a lady assistant told me that, though many attempts had been made to salvage what whisky remained in the ship, only a few bottles had been recovered. A diver had recovered a full bottle from the wreck but, when he opened it, the seawater had seeped in and it was ruined. She doubted if the wreck could still be seen, but I went to look anyway, half expecting to see the ship lying high and dry on a reef as it was depicted in the film, but the Sound was disappointingly empty and only a few gannets diving on a shoal of fish disturbed the glassy surface of the sea.

To finish the day, I had an enjoyable walk back to Acarsaid Mhor over Eriskay's highest hill, Ben Scrien, 185 metres, and with the tide well above the steps had no difficulty launching the dinghy. Two mature Irish ladies in a new motorsailer had picked up a vacant mooring close to *Halcyon* and they rowed over to ask if I could spare a carton of milk. I invited them aboard, and it made rather a hole in my stock of whisky, cans of lager, Pringle's crisps, and sausages and black pudding grilled on the stove, but they were delightful company, and the sun had long disappeared over the yardarm before we parted in a flurry of kisses and I was able to spread my sleeping bag on the deck.

Loch Lomond, Loch Ness, and to a lesser extent Loch Katrine in the Trossachs are forever being championed as the jewels in the Scottish landscape; yet on the eastern seaboard of the Hebrides there are long silent fjords hidden between hills, isolated, awkward to reach, difficult to penetrate and of a grandeur unsurpassed. I was bound for one of these when, after waving goodbye to the Irish ladies, I steered *Halcyon* away from Acarsaid Mhor on another amazingly flat calm, sunny morning, gave the coast a good offing to be clear of the inevitable sprinkling of Hebridean hazards, avoided the ferry terminal of Loch Boisdale and timed myself to be at the entrance to Loch Eynort in South Uist at low water.

Struthan Beag, the narrow entrance to Loch Eynort, is barred by a nasty elongated brute of a rock that is passable when uncovered and frightening when it is not, for the tidal stream boils over it at seven knots in a foaming rapid. I mistimed slack water slightly and had to give the engine full power to overcome the last spurt of the ebb, and it was with gritted teeth I crept slowly through the narrows and past the rock into Loch Eynort.

But my worries were by no means over. One of the perils of cruising in the Hebrides is that there are known submerged rocks you can see marked on the chart and lots of unknown ones you sometimes have the doubtful honour of discovering with your keel. Depth sounders are useless for rock spotting, and it is best to have someone standing in the bow to warn of any telltale streak of white below the surface. Those who sail alone are in the lap of the gods. With this thought in mind, I crept very cautiously into the comparatively shallow and chillingly rock-infested waters of Upper Loch Eynort, and anchored in a small sheltered bay on the south side.

It had been a nerve-rattling experience, but it was worth the effort. The mountain scenery that encircled the loch was incredible and in the evening, when the setting sun dipped towards the western horizon, bathing it in a deep red glow that gently merged into a velvety blackness until all that was left was a sky of twinkling stars, the only word that could possibly describe it was 'bewitching'.

I slept on deck again, and it was an exceptionally quiet night with not even the plop of a fish jumping. Radio reception was poor, though I managed to hear Radio Scotland's forecaster say that a low was approaching the Hebrides but the good weather would continue for a few more days. Having made several aborted attempts in past years to sail to St Kilda, a desolate group of islands way out in the

Atlantic forty miles west of the Sound of Harris, I had been fervently hoping that this would be my lucky year. The forecast low was not a good omen.

While breakfasting off the kippers I had bought in Castlebay, I studied the Ordnance Survey map to plan a walk in the hills and was surprised to find that the birthplace of Scotland's best-known heroine, Flora MacDonald, was only about four miles away, albeit with a hill in between and a river or two to cross; but it was a walk with a purpose and a chance to get to know the lovely island of South Uist. Not sure whether *Halcyon's* main anchor was dug into the sea bed or just clinging on to a clump of bladder wrack, I let go more chain and ran out the kedge anchor with a long warp astern.

Flora MacDonald's birthplace, South Uist

Rowing ashore and securing the dinghy above the high-water mark, I spread the map on a rock. It showed plenty of evidence of the Viking domination of the Hebrides in the names of the hills, Sheaval, Trinival and Arnaval; and there was a pass, though with a Gaelic name, Bealach Sheaval – the pass of Sheaval – cutting between Sheaval and Trinival. It seemed to be the quickest way to a track that would take me to the main road running the whole length of South and North Uist, and it was less than half a mile from the road to the ruin of Flora MacDonald's birthplace.

On the map it looked easy; but it was a long, wearying slog in deep heather up to the summit of the Bealach, and an equally exhausting scramble down the other side, followed by a splash across two burns and a squelch across heaving bog before

I reached the track leading to the scattered croft houses of Milton and a signpost that directed me down a narrow track to the ruin of a Tigh Dubh – black house, the traditional island thatched cottage – and a memorial that read:

> Flora MacDonald, daughter of Ranald son of Angus of Milton, South Uist. She was born in 1722 near this place and spent her early life in the house that stood on this foundation. When pursuit was drawing near to the Prince on the Long Island, she greatly aided him by her heroism and endurance to gain shelter in the Isle of Skye.

There is little doubt that the twenty-four-year-old Flora was an incredibly brave girl and worthy of the heroine status history has awarded her, but even the accounts of people who were with her at the time are not consistent. Whether she willingly assisted Bonnie Prince Charlie to escape capture by the English troops or whether family and friends pressured her into it is a tantalising riddle, to which there may never be an answer.

What historians do tell us is that after the disastrous failure of the Battle of Culloden near Inverness, the Prince was fleeing for his life with a £30,000 reward being offered for his capture, and by many gruelling routes he eventually reached South Uist, only a stone's throw from where, hardly a year earlier, he had landed in Eriskay.

Pursued by English troops, he was hiding with two friends, Captain O'Neil and Neil MacEachern, but an escape route had been planned for him by Flora's stepfather Hugh MacDonald, of Armadale in Skye, who, bizarrely, was in command of a company whose orders were to capture the Prince. Hugh MacDonald's plan was that Flora should return to her mother in Skye, taking with her the Prince disguised as a maid, with a prepared explanation that the maid was going into service with the family.

Apparently Flora was staying with her brother Angus at the family home, and, in a secret meeting in a hut nearby, met the Prince on the night of Friday, 20 June 1746. Captain O'Neil and Neil MacEachern outlined her stepfather's plan and asked if she would take part in it. Here the confusion arises. One eyewitness account of the meeting quotes Flora as saying that only with difficulty was she persuaded to take part in the plan. O'Neil says she refused on the ground that it would ruin a close friend, and yet, according to Neil MacEachern, 'She joyfully accepted of the offer without the least hesitation.'

Wherever the truth lies, we know that after a few frights, including Flora and MacEachern being arrested and released, the Prince, dressed as a maidservant, together with Flora MacDonald and Neil MacEachern, walked to Rossinish in Benbecula and was taken by boat across to Skye.

There were many tough times and near captures before the Prince was finally picked up by a French boat in Loch nan Uamh (nan-oo-a), near Arisaig on the mainland, and he sailed away never to see Scotland again. On their tour of Scotland, Dr Johnson and Boswell stayed with Flora and her husband, and Johnson wrote: 'We were entertained with the usual hospitality by Mr MacDonald and his lady, Flora MacDonald, a name that will be mentioned in history, and if courage and fidelity be virtues, with honour.'

It was an odd feeling to leave the ruin of the house perhaps on the same path the Prince had walked on after his meeting with Flora MacDonald, and what a story those old weathered stones could have told.

While I was enjoying my tea and sandwiches sitting on a rock, a couple who said they were on holiday from London arrived to take photographs of the Flora MacDonald monument. They told me proudly they had landed with their motor caravan by ferry at Loch Maddy on North Uist, driven down the new main road (without the faintest idea they had crossed over the island of Benbecula), and were on their way to Loch Boisdale to catch the ferry to Oban. They said they were not impressed with the bleakness of South Uist, but claimed to have 'done' the Hebrides.

What they had in fact done was miss a golden opportunity to get to know an island that on its west side has twenty miles of breathtakingly beautiful sandy beaches, where the rush-hour traffic is flocks of gulls flying in from the sea to roost, and which has a coastal machair (level grassland adjoining the beach) covered in wild flowers. Somehow they had even failed to notice the mountain splendour of Ben Mhor and Hecla, rising from the eastern shoreline to nearly 620 metres.

I returned to Loch Eynort and *Halcyon* by the same route through Mingary and, wet-footed and weary, squelched through bogs to Sheaval and the Bealach. The aerial view of the loch was outstanding, but I was relieved when it drew closer and I was eventually stretched out in the cockpit with a cooling can of lager, amused by the antics of a colony of seals who swam nervously around the boat, curious about the visitor from another world.

Regretting that the hot spell was coming to an end and that it would get cooler, the BBC's morning forecaster talked of a light westerly wind in the Hebrides, but at least it offered the first opportunity of using the sails since I had left the Clyde, and I hoisted the main and the mizzen to check the running rigging and hauled out the jib to test the roller reefing.

Having worked out a time to return through Struthan Beag narrows at high water when the tide was slack, I was reassured to see a few tidal swirls marking the position of the rock and, to keep well away from it, I hugged the shore on my port side as close as I dared and breathed a sigh of relief when the depth sounder climbed swiftly to twenty metres and I was in open sea. North from Eynort, the coast was rocky and forbidding, and with the promised westerly breeze never making it past the massif of Ben Mhor, Ben Corodale and Hecla, there was not so much as a wisp as I pointed *Halcyon* in the direction of Usinish Lighthouse, balanced on the top of a headland.

I was making for a gem of an anchorage known as the Wizard Pool in Loch Skipport at the top of South Uist, and had rounded Usinish Point and was steering for Ornish Island which marks the entrance to Skipport when, through binoculars, I spotted two girls in sea kayaks paddling towards *Halcyon* and waving furiously.

Savouring thoughts of hero status and hugs of adoration when I rescued them from the cruel sea (actually it was flat calm) I increased speed, but the dream faded when they turned out to be two lads with long hair held back in ponytails, and all they wanted was to ask if I could spare some water. They clung onto the deck stanchions while I filled their water containers, and with cheery waves and shouts of thanks went on their way, paddling for Loch Boisdale.

6

WIZARD POOL – HIGH ON HECLA – DIESEL DILEMMA

Entering Loch Skipport was nowhere near as testing as Loch Eynort and, apart from having to avoid a fish farm and a submerged rock, finding the way into the Wizard Pool was easy. By some magical means, the Wizard had cut a wide v-shaped notch into the rocky shoreline of the loch and conveniently plugged it with the boomerang-shaped island of Shillay Beag, on either side of which he had thoughtfully left a channel. Inside the pool he had provided himself with a tiny, heather-covered island to live on and, sounding my way in behind it, I let the anchor rattle down into three metres and was soon stretched out in the cockpit with a mug of coffee, soaking in the blissful atmosphere of the Wizard's lovely hideaway while my evening meal, a corned beef hash, bubbled away on the stove.

Who the Wizard was, or what happened to him, no one seems to know; but he would have made life a lot easier for sailing visitors to his haven had he waved his wand and cleared a space for dinghies to land on. Wherever I tried to land when I rowed ashore the next morning, I was faced with a minefield of sharp rocks concealed beneath slimy seaweed or steep knee-deep heather, and to prevent the dinghy being punctured I deflated it and carried it on my back to a safe place to leave it for the day.

I was on my way to climb Hecla, at 606 metres South Uist's second-highest mountain, pipped at the post by a mere fourteen metres by Ben Mhor, but no less impressive. I love sailing but I also enjoy climbing mountains and, as one of the ridges leading to Hecla's summit started quite literally from the Wizard Pool, it was a temptation too strong to resist.

The morning had dawned dry and sunny as forecast and it was a perfect day for a hill walk, though floundering through bogs and thick heather soon after leaving the pool was extremely tiring, and I was glad when the heather gave way to rock scrambling. There was no wind, and with the effort of the strenuous and unrelenting plod to the summit cairn my shirt was so soaked with sweat it dripped off me, but all the way the bird's-eye view of South Uist, looking north to Benbecula and North Uist and to the mountains of Harris, was incredible. To the west, ten miles out in the Atlantic I could clearly see the little-known Monach Islands, once the home of keepers who manned the lighthouse, but now deserted save for colonies of seabirds and seals. Hecla's rival, Ben Mhor, looked glorious a mile or so to the south and, in the pin-sharp visibility, the rocky headlands of the Isle of Skye coast and the white tower of Neist Point lighthouse, over twenty miles away, were crystal clear.

Only the occasional 'cronk, cronk' of a raven broke the silence, and I lay back against the summit cairn and thought about how precious the islands were, and how the unique character of the Hebrides and their special pace of life were in very real danger of being destroyed by over-exposure to tourism. No tourist organisation will ever accept that over-enthusiastic promotion of the islands could do more harm than good, and they argue that change is inevitable; but fortunately there are two forces of nature over which they have no control and which can be relied on to ensure a balance is maintained – the unpredictable weather and the fiendish midges.

Having a preference for a circular walk rather than retracing my steps, I descended Hecla's steep and rather daunting western ridge to flat moorland and found myself in a vast wilderness of bog, having to make endless detours to find a way through a network of tiny lochs. I floundered about for ages until, guided by *Halcyon's* main mast poking above the Wizard Pool, I eventually regained the dinghy. I inflated it with its pump and within minutes was back on board, dog-tired but elated by a memorable day on lovely South Uist.

Years of sailing in Hebridean waters, where there are often long distances between supplies of diesel, had taught me to fill as many spare containers as the boat could carry – short of stowing them under bunk mattresses – but having to rely on the engine all the way from the Clyde had almost used up my reserve.

Only a short distance from Loch Skipport was Loch Carnan, where environmentalists had accused the government of blighting the Uist landscape by building a huge oil-fired electricity generating station. To the islanders it was a godsend and, according to Martin Lawrence's indispensable *Yachtsman's Pilot to the Western Isles*, it would solve my fuel problem as well. It listed the oil terminal as a source of diesel for yachts.

A sketch plan in the *Pilot* showed a visitor's mooring conveniently close to the terminal so, sweeping the remnants of my breakfast toast over the side to a swan that had appeared from the direction of the island in the pool and could well have been the Wizard himself, I motored *Halcyon* round to Loch Carnan, picked up the mooring, went across to the oil terminal in the dinghy and presented myself at the office door with an array of plastic containers.

'Is it possible to have these containers filled with diesel?' said the office manager, echoing my question and looking with a glazed expression at the giant oil storage tanks in the yard, then back at the plastic fuel cans. 'Not a hope!' he exploded. 'This is the supply point for the power station, not the bloody island garage. Who told you to come here anyway?'

I explained, but he was not impressed. 'Well, I don't know where he got that information from. We don't supply yachts here. I can't help you. Sorry.' And with that he turned and strode back to his office.

All my life I had found that islanders would go to great lengths to help strangers in need; and, feeling at a complete loss, I was lowering the containers into the dinghy when he suddenly appeared again with a big smile on his face. 'You're in luck,' he beamed, 'I hate to see you stuck, so I've been in touch with one of the road tankers that delivers fuel to the crofts, and if you are prepared to wait an hour he'll supply you with diesel.' It was marvellous news and in due course the tanker arrived, squirted a hundred and fifty litres of the engine's life blood into the containers, and I returned to *Halcyon* with my faith in the islanders restored.

Halcyon's mooring was draped in thick weed and probably had not been checked for years, but the weather was still settled and I decided to stay overnight and plan my route ahead. The island next to South Uist was Benbecula. About six miles long and roughly circular, it looked like a stepping stone conveniently placed to enable giants to step from South to North Uist without getting their feet wet. For centuries, lesser mortals had been obliged to make the journey by crossing tidal fords at the extreme ends of Benbecula, and there were many gruesome tales of travellers being swept away while attempting the crossing at the wrong time.

In 1960 the journey was made easier when the Queen Mother opened a causeway across to North Uist, and in the 1980s a concrete causeway was opened connecting South Uist. The local economy was given a boost by the establishment of a Royal Artillery missile range in South Uist in 1957, and tourism was helped along by another book from Sir Compton Mackenzie, *Rockets Galore*. It was also made into a film, but I thought it was nothing like as funny as *Whisky Galore*.

It was on Benbecula that Prince Charlie hid in a cave for three days in June 1746, while Flora MacDonald was collecting the female clothing in which the Prince made his escape as the maidservant 'Betty Burke'. Wedged between the two Uists, Benbecula is the unofficial line that separates the Catholic islands of the south from the Protestant north, though in the Western Isles the two have lived and intermingled with each other peacefully for centuries, and there are no communities bedecked with national flags, provocative slogans and anti-religious graffiti. Seen from the sea, the points where Benbecula starts and ends are lost in a labyrinth of smaller islands that hide delightful anchorages; but, though I was tempted to linger, my thoughts were on reaching St Kilda and, conscious of the approaching low-pressure system I left Loch Carnan, bound for Loch Maddy in North Uist where I wanted to visit the nearby island of Berneray.

Just as the morning forecaster on Radio Scotland said it would, a chilly south-westerly breeze sprang up, and for the first time in weeks I was able to hoist all sails, but it was slow progress. I was leaving the Sea of the Hebrides and entering the Minch, another lively expanse of Western Isles water renowned for relieving ferry passengers of their breakfast, and a strong tidal stream heading south almost cancelled the power of the wind. Three hours after leaving Loch Carnan I had barely covered six nautical miles.

Loch Carnan Power Staion, South Uist

Off the island of Ronay, at the southern end of North Uist, the wind died completely, and before the tide could sweep me back I started the engine, engaged the autopilot and lashed down the sails. The wind returned with an extra punch an hour later when I was abeam of Loch Eport, but it had veered to the north and, with only three miles to go to reach Loch Maddy, I had no enthusiasm for hauling up the heavy gaff mainsail again. Convincing myself that when a man is in his seventies he has every right to opt for using the engine, I escaped the rigours of a thrash to windward and, in a fraction of the time it would have taken me under sail, I was rolling gently on a mooring close to Loch Maddy's ferry terminal, enjoying a mug of hot coffee.

It was while filling the kettle to make coffee that I discovered the water tanks were very low, and later in the afternoon I rowed across to MacBrayne's office on the ferry pier to ask if I could use their water hose. 'Of course you can,' said a smiling lady at the reception desk. 'Just you bring your wee boat across to the pier, I'm sure one of the shore crew will help you.'

Back at *Halcyon*, I slipped the mooring and motored across to the pier where one of the shore men secured my warps. Forty years had gone by since I had lived on the island of Lewis, and foolishly I tried out the limited Gaelic I had picked up while I was there and asked him if he would help me to fill the tanks with water. He gave me a puzzled look and said he hadn't got any, and I thought he was being unhelpful as he was standing next to a coiled hose and a tap.

When I asked again in English, he burst out laughing. Apparently I had asked him for whisky! I half expected a chorus of wisecracks from MacBrayne's staff lined up on the pier as I sheepishly returned *Halcyon* to the mooring, but true native islanders are too polite to ridicule visitors to their face. Having helped me to fill the tanks, all the man said when he cast the warps off was 'Enjoy your sailing,' though I'm quite sure in the hotel bar that night there were roars of laughter, and he earned a few free drinks telling the story of the bodach (old man) in the wooden boat with the red sails who wanted to fill his water tanks with whisky!

One normally constant feature of the Hebrides is the wind, yet the glossy brochures published by the Western Isles Tourist Board seldom mention it. A function of the Tourist Information Offices on the islands appears to be to convince holidaymakers that the sun is always shining on their chosen destination; that woeful tales about biting midges are a dastardly invention of the English Tourist Board; and the skin-soaking Scotch mist is only in the imagination of poets. Any reference to the wind is diplomatically avoided and yet, unless the weather is exceptional, the wind, usually from the west or south-west, is always there, and up to reaching North Uist I had been amazingly lucky. But, at sunset, a south-westerly blow moaned around *Halcyon* and it was a reminder that I was in a region that held the British record for gales; and to drive home the point it blew hard all night and kept me awake.

Much to my relief, at about 5 a.m. it suddenly became calm, and by 8 a.m. the sun was out, the sky was blue and the air warm. The weather lady's explanation on the radio was that we had been on the receiving end of a vicious low-pressure system that had charged in from the Atlantic, but was now on its way to stir up the seas around Orkney and Shetland. She said the exceptional weather Scotland had been enjoying would continue for at least another week, but added we should make the most of it while we could.

In the Hebrides there are a confusing number of islands called Berneray, but perhaps the most captivating of them all lies off the tip of North Uist. While I was in MacBrayne's office to ask about filling up with water, I had picked up a local bus timetable and leaflets about the island and was surprised to discover that, since my last visit, the island ferry had been replaced by a causeway.

Attaching the Scottish islands to each other or to the mainland with a permanent umbilical cord had always been a bone of contention, and when the controversial bridge was built across to the island of Skye there was a voluble lobby that argued Skye was no longer an island. I had some sympathy with the campaign but, like opening the floodgates of tourism, if that is what the islanders want then that should be the end of the argument.

I often wonder, though, if radical change is the wish of the native islanders or of the incomers, intolerant of island tradition. A lady I sat next to on the bus from Loch Maddy to Berneray the next morning had no hesitation in telling me that the causeway was the best thing that could have happened to the island, though she did admit reluctantly that it had led to an annoying increase in tourist traffic along roads not designed to take it. 'It's those fancy caravan motors,' she complained, 'some of them are bigger than this bus!'

Hebridean islands always look their best when the sky is blue and the sun is shining, and the first impression most visitors to Berneray get is how green it is. One of the reasons is that, unlike most other Hebridean islands, Berneray does not have any peat; instead it is covered with a sandy soil, ideal for growing crops and maintaining rich grazing land.

The guide leaflet recommended that I explored the east side of the island first, probably with the object of channelling visitors in the direction of the island's shops, so I left the bus as soon as it crossed to the island and enjoyed a pleasant walk through tiny communities where colourful new houses had sprung up alongside the old 'black houses'.

What interested me more than anything was a new concrete harbour that had been built in Bays Loch, the main settlement. It opened on to the Sound of Harris and I could see it would be a very useful place to stop on my way back from St Kilda. I was busy photographing it when the lady I had sat with on the bus came walking along the quay. 'You should have a look at the Giant's Monument,' she called, 'it's well worth a photograph. Go back past the harbour, then take the road to Borve. The machair is amazing along there.'

The road to the Borve machair passed between two rows of incredibly modern houses that looked slightly incongruous in their island setting. In almost a whisper, my helpful lady friend had informed me that another Bonnie Prince Charlie, this one the son of our reigning Queen, had stayed secretly in one of them in the 1980s. To 'get away from it all' and experience something of real life, the royal advisers had sent Charles to Berneray, and he was taken lobster fishing, worked on the crofts, handled sheep, got to know local people and probably had the most enjoyable time of his life. Beyond the smart houses, the road ended at one of the loveliest expanses of wildflower-covered machair I had ever seen in my life, and the white, sandy beach running along the west coast was so breathtaking it almost defied

The Giant's Monument – Berneray, North Uist

description. In his marvellous book *The Scottish Islands*, Hamish Haswell-Smith describes it as 'four kilometres of perfection'.

Walking back along the machair to catch the bus to return to Loch Maddy, I stopped at the intriguing monument to Angus MacAskill, the Berneray giant, who was reputed to be 2.36 metres tall; and a crofter who was preparing to plough part of the machair with a tractor told me he was born on Berneray in 1825, but his parents emigrated to Nova Scotia when he was six.

In later years, because of his enormous height he was something of a freak and was in show business. 'I've heard it said he toured with the midget, Tom Thumb, who used to dance on the palm of his hand, but I don't know if there's any truth in it,' said the crofter cautiously. 'He never returned to Berneray and died of a fever when he was only thirty-eight.' To give an impression of the giant's height, the monument was 2.36 metres high, and surrounded by a wall built of pebbles from the beach.

Catching a last glimpse of the island through the window of the bus as it drove away, I could see why Berneray could boldly claim to be one of the most interesting and beautiful islands in the Hebrides; but with an increasing population attracted by the 'good life', and well established on the 'tourist trail', I felt it could soon become a victim of it own popularity.

7

GATEWAY TO ST KILDA – TARANSAY – THE DOOK'S CASTLE

Loch Maddy (Loch nam Madadh – the loch of the dogs) got its name from two dog-shaped rocks, Madadh Beag and Madadh Mor, at the entrance to the loch, and they were a welcome sight to the crew when I worked on the fishing boats in my youth. It meant a few hours undisturbed sleep, and eating a meal without being thrown all over the boat by the sea. The locals liked to tell that Loch Maddy was once the haunt of pirates who preyed on shipping, but in more settled times the many islands scattered around the loch have become the breeding ground of hundreds of seabirds and wildfowl, and a paradise for bird watchers.

Its reputation as a sheltered anchorage for yachts was tested during the night, when the wind the weather lady said had gone to the Northern Isles had obviously decided it liked the Hebrides better, and returned with a vengeance to rock *Halcyon* with some hefty gusts and batter the coach roof with bursts of heavy rain. By morning it was still quite fresh from the south and raining steadily, and outside the loch I could see white-capped waves rolling up the Minch.

With the entrance to the Sound of Harris, 'the Gateway to St Kilda', only nine miles up the coast, I would soon have to decide whether it was feasible to enter the Sound and commit myself to a single-handed forty-mile thrash out into the unpredictable Atlantic, to a group of islands where there was absolutely no shelter. It was not a decision to be taken lightly, and I ducked out of making it by opting to anchor for the night in Loch Rodel at the entrance to the Sound and hope that the evening forecast would provide some encouraging news.

Hoisting the mizzen and jib and leaving the main lashed down, I let go the mooring and scudded out of Loch Maddy, passing Madadh Beag to port in a flurry of spray as waves broke against *Halcyon*'s side. Once clear of the loch, the wind was gusting at the top end of force six (twenty-five knots) and the sea was rough, but wind and tide were in my favour and, with a couple of rolls in the jib and the mizzen eased out, *Halcyon* rode the following seas very comfortably. Occasionally an extra-violent rain squall dipped the port side deck into the water, and hanging on to the tiller with my feet braced against the cockpit seat was like sailing a racing dinghy, but thanks to the buoyancy of *Halcyon*'s wide beam she soon righted herself.

A large rusty freighter, flying the flag of Panama, came up astern and kept me company as I surfed across the mouth of the Sound of Harris, and then it forged ahead and disappeared very quickly in the direction of the Shiant Isles, leaving me crashing through breaking seas off Renish Point when I turned into Loch Rodel. I had reached the island of Harris (Na Hearadh – the High Land), and with rain clouds hanging low over the hills it was a darker and more forbidding landscape than the Uists, though with its own particular character and charm.

The passage through the Sound of Harris, which separates North Uist from Harris, can be a nightmare or an exciting navigational challenge, depending on how confident you are about venturing into a vast maze of islands, islets, rocks and shallow passages swept by erratic tidal streams that constantly change direction and play havoc with even the most carefully prepared route plan.

About ten miles long by roughly eight wide, the Sound has two main navigable channels, the Stanton Channel on the Harris side and the Cope Channel on the North Uist side. The passage through the Stanton Channel is in deep water, but relies on being able to identify sometimes difficult to see transits and is at the mercy of strong cross-tides. The Cope Channel threads through a labyrinth of small islets and drying rocks, and would have been impossible without local knowledge had it not been for the Army, who made it safer for their landing craft carrying stores to the radar station at St Kilda by laying a line of port and starboard buoys from the Minch on the east side to the Atlantic on the west.

It earned them the undying gratitude of fishing boat skippers and visiting yacht crews; though, having cleared the channel, the navigator still has a final obstacle. A notorious sandbank, hidden under shallow water that has been known to dry out, bars the way to the ocean, and if any wind is opposed to the tide it can kick up a wicked sea.

Despite its evil reputation, many cruising yacht skippers are discovering that, in settled weather, the Sound of Harris is no more hazardous than many other passages in the Hebrides; and for those with St Kilda and the seldom-visited west side of the Hebrides on their 'must see' list there are few alternatives. And so it was towards the bright green number one buoy at the start of the channel that I steered *Halcyon*, under engine, the following morning to catch the flood, after a quiet night anchored in Loch Rodel.

The wind had dropped to a mere murmur of a breeze, and though Stornoway Coastguard's early morning bulletin indicated that the weather was not to be as settled as I had hoped for, it had at least given me the confidence to go through the Sound and spend a few days exploring the islands and anchorages on the west coast of Harris. From there I could assess the weather prospects and decide whether I dared to risk the exposed eighty-mile round trip into the capricious Atlantic.

The tidal stream seemed determined to push *Halcyon* across the channel and onto the rocks, but it was no match for the power of the engine and I made steady progress, ticking off the buoys as I passed until, leaving the island of Berneray to port, I cleared a large yellow buoy marking the end of the Cope Channel and set a course for the tiny island of Coppay, a lone sentinel at the north-west corner of the Sound.

The sky was grey and overcast, and I was pleased that there was only a light wind behind a long swell rolling in from the west, though *Halcyon* thudded heavily into the troughs, sending spray flying into the air and rattling the pans in the galley. From leaving the Cope Channel it took two hours to reach Coppay, and after being thrown about violently it was a relief to round the formidable cliffs of Toe Head on Harris and escape the swell in the sheltered bay of Camus nam Borgh.

Switching the engine off I let *Halcyon* drift while I went below, made a mug of coffee and sat in the cockpit admiring the lovely island of Taransay close to the shore. It still had the air of detached serenity I remembered from the time I landed on it from a fishing boat in 1950 and strolled among the abandoned houses and the school. I felt very sad when it was pitched into the glare of publicity while being invaded by a group of people chosen by a television company to play a survival game.

I watched a few of the episodes of the TV series out of curiosity and to see Taransay again, but the 'castaways' were horribly ill-prepared for a world beyond their normal, mundane, urban life. The ghosts of Saint Taran and the hardy men and women who had survived on Taransay for centuries must have watched their antics with considerable bewilderment, and been appalled by the bickering of the 'new islanders' as they struggled to live together.

The tide was just right for going through Taransay Sound into West Loch Tarbert, and I was keen to reach the small but sheltered and picturesque anchorage of Loch Leosavay on its north side, where I intended to anchor. Starting the engine I lined up the transits that would take me clear of submerged rocks between Taransay and Harris, and a touch over an hour later, having gone through the Sound and rounded the islands of Soay Mor and Soay Beag that straddle the seaward entrance to West Loch Tarbert, *Halcyon* was swinging to her anchor in Loch Leosavay.

I hung a fishing line over the side and boiled a few potatoes and carrots for dinner, which to my delight were soon joined by a big fat mackerel. The evening weather bulletins of Stornoway Coastguard and the BBC, if not gloomy, were not encouraging, with a forecast of unsettled conditions in the west of Scotland and the possibility of strengthening wind accompanied by rain. Any hopes I had of sailing to St Kilda were fading fast, but for the present I was in a perfect anchorage and it was blissfully peaceful. I had enjoyed a good meal and a good read, and when it had become dark I climbed into my sleeping bag and slept through the night completely undisturbed.

A peculiar hissing noise and repeated thumps against the hull had me leaping out of my bunk and into the cockpit at 7 a.m., just in time to see the tails of two otters diving under *Halcyon* after fish. I dashed below to get my camera but they had gone when I got back on deck, so I inflated the dinghy and, when breakfast was over, rowed ashore, hoping to stock up with fresh food at a small shop I had noticed on the edge of the loch.

Two friendly American ladies busy writing postcards outside the shop asked if I was 'the guy from the sailboat in the bay', and when I said 'yes' the elder of the two reached in her handbag and produced a wad of photographs of a boat very similar to *Halcyon*, and said that she and her late husband had built it in Florida and sailed it up and down the east coast of America and out to the Bahamas. 'Charlie and me worked our butts off for over two years buildin' that sailboat,' she declared proudly. 'We sailed it thousands of miles and had us a great time till he got sick and died. Ah sure do miss the sonofabitch!'

It had started to rain steadily and I stood under a nearby lean-to, leafing slowly through the photographs of a wooden boat in various stages of construction; the launch day when the boat and everything around it seemed to be festooned with the American flag, and shots of her husband and herself in shorts and T-shirts relaxing on deck in the sun, eating ice cream. 'It's not a day for eating ice cream on my boat,' I laughed, handing her the photographs back, 'and it would be hard work trying to build a wooden boat outdoors in Scotland. We could do with some of your Florida weather!'

'I guess so,' she smiled, 'but if you had the weather you wouldn't have the unique atmosphere of the islands and the hills, with the mist and the deer and all. We ain't got nothing like it in the States. We ain't got no castles either.' Gesturing towards the gaunt bulk of Amhuinnsuidhe (Avan-soo-ee) Castle, a large stone-built house with a turret that dominated the landscape above the loch, she went on, 'My friend here discovered that even this goddam hotel we're staying in is a castle a dook built for his lady.'

'Sure did,' her friend agreed, 'and it's so romantic I can hardly wait to tell the folks back home.'

The rain began to pour in torrents and, suddenly remembering they had booked a car to take them on a tour of Harris, they thrust their postcards into the mail box and set off towards the castle. 'Have a nice day,' they called. 'Hope this lousy weather clears up for you.'

'And for you,' I shouted back.

As I sheltered from the rain and watched them go, I felt I should have told them that the real history of the castle is far from being a romantic story; but it would have tarnished the starry-eyed image they had of the 'dook' and his lady. I had read a lot about Amhuinnsuidhe and the ladies would have been very disappointed to learn that it was built not by a Duke but by an Earl, a title several notches below a Duke in the British aristocratic pecking order.

The location of Loch Leosavay is so breathtakingly spectacular it is the perfect setting for a house, and Charles, 7th Earl of Dunmore, who owned Harris in 1867, thought so too, and ploughed a fortune into building a country retreat for his wife Gertrude, the daughter of the Earl of Leicester. Unhappily for the Earl, she was a lady with expensive tastes who preferred the social life of London and was not very enamoured with her husband's passion for spending time in his Hebridean wilderness. Desperate to prove to his lady that the Harris rain, the lively ferry crossing from the mainland, the gales, the appalling roads of the time and the midges could be just as endearing as the continual round of parties, gossip, intrigue and fashionable balls that were the London season, he poured his heart and his cash into a flamboyant castle and gave it the rather lovely name of Amhuinnsuidhe which, in Gaelic, means 'Sitting by the River'.

The American ladies might have been won over by the story so far and thrilled by the Earl's devotion to his wife, but it would have ruined their holiday to hear that, when the hard-hearted Gertrude was taken to see the finished castle, she shattered her husband's dream by scathingly dismissing his token of affection for her, saying 'it wasn't as big as a hen house or a stable at her father's house'. Poor Charles must have despaired of his demanding wife but, still frantic to please her, he had an extra wing built on the castle. Alas, she was still unimpressed; worse, the castle drained away all his cash and he went bust. Huge amounts of money had been lavished on Amhuinnsuidhe, yet no member of the Dunmore family ever enjoyed the pleasure of living in it.

The Earl's bankers sold the castle and numerous notable people have since owned it, including Sir Tom Sopwith, the flying ace. In 1913 James Barrie, the author of *Peter Pan*, stayed there and was inspired to write his play *Mary Rose*. In 2003, the 55,000 acre North Harris estate, which included the castle, was bought in a joint bid of over £4 million by the residents of North Harris and a businessman, Ian Scarr-Hall. The shooting rights were leased back to Mr Scarr-Hall, who also bought the castle and the fishing rights. The castle is now an exclusive and superbly appointed country hotel.

Donald Angus, my old shipmate on the fishing boats, used to say there were three things a visitor to Harris should not miss, Amhuinnsuidhe Castle, the island of Scarp, and the Norwegian whaling station in Loch Bunavoneadar at the head of

West Loch Tarbert. A study of the chart showed that Bunavoneadar was only five miles away and, preferring to be on the move in pouring rain rather than be cooped up in the cabin, I pulled on my oilies, started the engine, heaved up the anchor, and towing the dinghy astern ploughed a furrow through the grey water of the loch.

There was no wind and the rain had pushed the cloud down low on the hills, making visibility patchy. The chunky islands of Soay Mor and Soay Beg in the middle of the loch were easy to identify, but I stared ahead trying in vain to spot a group of four islets called Duisker that were mere pinpricks on the chart. My Gaelic dictionary was little help with the meaning of Duisker but I found that duis (doosh) meant mist. About a mile further up the loch the Gaels must have baffled the Admiralty chart-makers by calling another prominent rock Duisker, but I never saw either of them and if there is a Gaelic word that means Lost in the Mist it would suit them better.

Despite the restricted visibility there were no hazards entering Loch Bunavoneadar. A conspicuous chimney mentioned in the Pilot Book was an ideal beacon and easy to see in the torrential rain, and I dropped anchor close to an old slipway and rowed ashore. It was a dismal day and hopeless for photography, but there was little left to photograph anyway. Donald Angus had told me that the whaling station had been established by the Norwegians before the 1914–18 war, and was bought by Lord Leverhulme, the soap magnate, in 1920.

He saw it as a useful addition to a fish-processing enterprise he had built in the Sound of Harris, and chartered three Norwegian whaling ships to keep the plant supplied. His intention was to transport the extracted oil to his soap-manufacturing empire at Port Sunlight, near Liverpool, and use the whale meat to make sausages for exporting to Africa. There was no limit to Leverhulme's enthusiasm and determination to create industry and employment for the islanders; but, although over 6,000 tons of meat were processed, the venture never caught on and in 1930 the station closed down. It was re-opened by the Norwegians in 1950 and Donald Angus was hoping to give up the hard life on the fishing boats and get a permanent job with them; but before he was taken on the venture was declared uneconomical and the buildings and plant abandoned to plunderers and the ravages of the weather.

I wandered round what I thought would have been the processing site, but the only trace left was the crumbling slipway, some steps and the chimney. Given that the world has at last developed a conscience about the destruction of whales, it was not a place to be glorified but, if the chimney was the original one built before the 1914–18 war, it was a monument to its builders and seemed worthy of listed building status.

Back on board, I made a lunch of hot soup and coffee and unfolded an Ordnance Survey map of the area. Loch Bunavoneadar was well sheltered and lay at the foot of Clisham, at 799 metres the highest mountain in Harris, and had it been a fine,

Clisham, Harris
stands at
799 metres

clear day it would have been a perfect opportunity to leave *Halcyon* safely at anchor and climb it. But the low cloud hung like a thick curtain over the landscape and the rain showed no sign of easing. Clisham would have to wait for another day.

The cloud was still low and the visibility poor when I dropped anchor off Amhuinnsuidhe again and the damp, humid conditions were perfect for that scourge of all Scottish Tourist Boards, *Culicoides impunctatus*, the Scottish midge. One of the species of biting midges, biting is their speciality, and with gnashing teeth, they swarmed in millions through every door and ventilator on *Halcyon*, and life in the cabin was miserable. They devoured the midge repellent on my face and arms as though it was chocolate fudge and, desperately searching through lockers for anything that would relieve the burning pain, I discovered a box of mosquito coils.

The instructions promised that, once ignited, the contents would protect the user from all biting insects, and though it was alarming to read that they were for outdoor use only and I should not breathe the smoke, I had reached the stage where I would rather die of asphyxiation than be eaten alive by these flying carnivores. Desperate for rapid results, I lit two coils instead of the recommended one, and within minutes thick, acrid smoke spiralled upwards and the interior of the cabin was like a kippering plant. I was choking for breath, but so were the midges, and in a flash they stampeded for the fresh air and were gone.

When I covered the coils and opened all the hatches I half expected the onslaught to return, but word must have got around and I was left in peace. I spent an uncomfortable night though, gingerly dabbing painful flesh with anti-histamine cream and vigorously scratching parts of me where no self-respecting midge ought to have ventured.

Unable to sleep, I crawled on deck draped in my sleeping bag like a duvet quilt, and at first light watched the newborn Hebridean day emerge from the night. The clouds had lifted and were spread across the hilltops like a gigantic grey blanket, and a pale sun was doing its best to climb over it into the sky. It was low tide, and on the shore a large red deer stag and a group of hinds nibbled cautiously at seaweed, and there was not a sound save for the occasional squabbling oystercatcher and the cry of a lapwing. The American lady was right. The vagaries of Scotland's weather had lots of compensations.

Splashes in the water and a thump against *Halcyon*'s hull were signs that the otters were harassing the mackerel again, and when I hung a line over the side I was quickly rewarded with a couple of fish for breakfast. When the sun had warmed the air I ate them in the cockpit, freshly grilled, with buttered toast and fresh coffee. Basking in the sun and feeling *Halcyon* rock gently with the movement of the tide was idyllic, but Stornoway Coastguard's morning weather bulletin spoilt it by revealing that the low-pressure system they had been warning about, but which had remained stationary out in the Atlantic, was now on the move again. It seemed I had but a few days more to see as much of the west coast of Harris and Lewis as I could, and I spread out the charts to plan a route.

The third of Donald Angus's trio of 'must see' places in Harris was the island of Scarp and, by good fortune, the island and Caolas an Scarp, the narrow stretch of water that separated it from Harris and provided access to lochs beyond, was barely five miles away, close to the entrance to West Loch Tarbert. Caolas an Scarp was shallow, and to safely cross a sandbar at its narrowest point I would have to be there about half flood. There was a light wind from the south-west that would take me through very nicely.

The only real problems were three extensive patches of rocks to steer clear of before I reached Caolas an Scarp: Taransay Glorigs and Huisinis Glorigs, with a channel about two miles wide between them, and a nasty group called Old Rocks further to the west. My Gaelic dictionary offered no help with the meaning of 'glorig,' but they were dangerous hazards and might be difficult to see if there was any swell running, so I sailed from Loch Leosavay with a line of plots on the chart that would keep me well away from them.

There was a moderate swell, probably caused by the forecasted approaching low-pressure area out in the Atlantic but, despite a roller-coaster ride, I made good time under all sail. The seas were breaking with tremendous force on Huisinis Glorigs and on Old Rocks, sending spray high into the air, and I was glad when I rounded the cliffs of Huisinis Point; but even in the entrance to Caolas an Scarp the sea was white and confused so, to prevent a gybe at the wrong time, I hove to and dropped the mainsail. Steering was much easier under mizzen and jib, and in the lee of Scarp I was able to drop anchor off an old stone jetty and row ashore.

8

ROCKET POST – A SEAL CONVENTION – SAIL PROBLEMS

Scarp (An Sgarp in Gaelic) is said to mean 'barren' and the hilly island is certainly that, with just a few houses crowded close to the pier and the island burial ground. The community once had a population of over two hundred, and a handful clung on until the 1970s when they too finally gave up the struggle to survive and moved to Harris. A few holidaymakers used the croft houses in the summer months, but the reality was that Scarp had become another casualty on the long list of abandoned and lifeless Hebridean islands where families had been born, lived and died, psalms had been sung in the church, tweed had been woven, fish cured for the winter on a line like clothes hanging out to dry, and peat smoke had once drifted up from the cluster of croft houses.

The island's name was etched firmly on the world map in the 1930s, when Gerhard Zucker, a German rocket enthusiast, hit the headlines by attempting to send letter post over to Harris from the island by rocket. Having been successful in firing a rocket with a payload of letters across the Sussex Downs in England, he wanted to impress the Royal Mail by firing one from an island. Why he chose remote Scarp is not clear but, at the end of July 1934, having decided it was the ideal site for his experiment, he set up his rocket, packed with letters, ready for the first rocket mail delivery to Harris.

It excited widespread interest and special stamps were printed for the occasion and letters written to dignitaries and to King George V. Politicians and top brass from the Royal Mail made the arduous journey from London to watch the event, and might well have joined in the chorus of the countdown; but when the proud inventor lit the fuse, instead of soaring across the Sound, the rocket exploded and scattered charred letters over the hillside. Taking his job seriously, the island post-master gathered them up and unwittingly turned them into highly valuable and sought-after collectors' items by writing on them, 'Damaged by explosion at Scarp, Harris'.

Undaunted, Zucker set up another rocket, at Huisinis on Harris and this time the Scarp rocket post was successful, but the confidence and the credibility of the politicians who had supported him had been undermined and, to save losing face, they branded the ill-fated inventor a 'threat to the income of the post office and the security of the country' and deported him to Germany. Had Zucker's experiment been a success, he would probably have been hailed a hero and a monument to his achievement erected on Scarp, but I could not find as much as a plaque. A very poignant film called *The Rocket Post* was made about it in 2001 which strayed into a fantasy story; but for anyone curious to see what the west side of Harris looks like, the photography of the Sounds and the islands is phenomenal.

I would have enjoyed spending the day exploring Scarp, but there was a swell crashing against the shore and, worried about leaving *Halcyon* unattended at anchor, I had a quick wander among the silent cottages and went back on board to study the charts and decide on a safe anchorage for the night. I was on the invisible border line between Harris and Lewis, and beyond Scarp the landscape and the seascape were wild and desolate.

The shore was mountainous with no habitation, no shop, no fuel, no water – except from burns on the hills – no mobile phone reception, very broken VHF contact with the Coastguard, and BBC radio reception that faded. There was only a faint possibility of anyone seeing a flare if you fired one off, almost no buoys or lights and plenty of unmarked rocks. Marinas were unheard of, and sudden changes of weather and sea conditions frequent.

Most important of all, there was little chance of finding help if anything went wrong. Not surprisingly, there are not many sails to be seen around; but for all its dangers and disadvantages, the west side of Harris and Lewis is hauntingly beautiful and the sea lochs are a cruising sailor's dream. It makes the dream even pleasanter to have a good pilot book, and both Imray's *Western Isles* Pilot by Martin Lawrence and the Admiralty Pilot give a host of good advice about anchorages and navigation directions beyond Scarp.

The north end of Caolas an Scarp is partially blocked by the island of Fladday, and I changed my plan to go through a channel on its east side when I saw it was a mass of white-topped waves and the chart showed there were submerged rocks. I went the long way round by the west channel to pick up the tiny island of Greine Sgeir and steer a course from it directly into Loch Cravadale, and a quiet anchorage close to a lovely sandy beach. A slight swell followed me in, but it was bearable and sheltered by the grey bulk of Husival Mor, a hill that filled the head of the bay. I was out of the wind and enjoyed the warmth of the sun.

It was a perfect evening for dining ashore and, loading the dinghy with one of those small portable barbecues that only need a match to get them going, I added canned sausages, canned beefburgers and tomatoes. With a cake for dessert and a bottle of wine to wash the lot down, I rowed ashore and sat on the brilliant white sand enjoying a fine meal. The only thing missing was female company; that, like the other services essential to a cruising sailor, was hard to find in a Hebridean wilderness.

The Ordnance Survey map of the area showed a freshwater loch, Loch a' Ghlinne, close to the shore with an outlet running into the bay, and in the evening sun I walked up to have a look at it. Nearly two miles long, it nestled in the spectacular, narrow, high-sided ravine of Glen Cravadale. There was neither a soul to be seen nor a sound to be heard, and as I crunched along a stalker's path on the north side of the loch, I felt I was intruding on the solitude. It was one of those magical places that could only be reached from a boat or after a long walk through the hills, and it was what made Harris and Lewis so special.

Retracing my steps to where the loch poured into the sea, I stripped off and lathered myself from head to foot with a bar of soap brought for the purpose. To conserve my precious 300 litres of drinking water on board I never wasted it on body washing, resorting instead to using a bucket of seawater and seawater soap that guaranteed a lather despite the salt content of the water. The disadvantage of washing in sea water was that the salt tended to dry on my skin and at the end of a week or so, whenever I took my clothes off salt cascaded onto the floor as though I had burst a packet of crisps. Wallowing in fresh water to wash the salt away, then pulling on clean dry clothes, was a rare luxury and I was a new man. Gathering up the dinner debris I rowed back to *Halcyon* to decide on a route for the following day.

The chart showed there were three lochs left to explore in the vicinity of Scarp, Loch Resort, Loch Tealasavay and Loch Tamanavay, with a possible visit to Mealista Island about half a mile off the Lewis coast. My fishermen pals used to joke that anyone born on Mealista grew up to be half-witted, but the island had been abandoned some time in the 19th century so it was probably a cruel rumour that might have had a lot to do with a dodgy water supply or inbreeding due to the island's isolation.

From Mealista it was only ten miles north to the fabulous cruising ground of Loch Roag, where it was possible to explore inlets and islands under sail for a week and still not uncover all its secrets. Having never visited it by boat, I was tempted to make a run for Loch Roag, but I knew the ten miles from Mealista Island to Loch Roag had a coastline of huge cliffs and a reputation for heavy swell, outlying rocks, and seas that could rapidly become treacherous. In other words, for a small boat the weather for the passage had to be very settled, and the Atlantic low on its way hardly promised that.

I could not receive Stornoway Coastguard on VHF and the BBC's late-night shipping forecast was a bit garbled, but from it I managed to glean the warming news that the low was tracking further north than expected and the wind force in the Hebrides would be a lot less than originally thought. The bad news was it was to veer to the north-west, which meant it would be blowing directly into Loch Cravadale. By 7 a.m. the next morning it had reached fifteen knots (force four) and *Halcyon* was gyrating wildly at the end of the anchor chain.

The movement in the cabin was too lively to eat breakfast and, anxious to find shelter, I went on deck to raise the anchor. The chain was bar-taut with the strain, and it took a lot of furious cranking at the winch and rushing into the cockpit to surge the boat forward under engine before the anchor lifted off the bottom and I could drive forward into deep water to have enough sea room to heave it on board. Under mizzen and jib *Halcyon* sailed sedately into the long narrow fjord of Loch Resort, and I was startled to see a fishing boat heading towards me.

It was the first sign of life I had seen since leaving Loch Leosavay, and the skipper seemed as surprised to see me as I was at seeing him when he steered his boat alongside and asked where I had come from. We talked for a while, and he advised me not to go through Caolas an Scarp if the wind was strong from the north and said that I would find it sheltered in Loch Resort. 'The loch is deep,' he advised, 'but Dirascal is a good place to anchor on the south side, or you can go right to the head of the loch. Put plenty of chain out, mind; you can get the squalls coming off the hills when the wind is from the north.'

He spoke in Gaelic to his crewman who delved into a fish box and handed me four fish about the size of a trout, 'cuddies' he called them. 'Something for your tea,' grinned the skipper, and with a shout to his crewman to cast off the warps tied to *Halcyon*, he revved his engine and steamed away down the loch.

Dirascal was about two miles further up the loch, tucked away in a small bay, and though there were indications it had at some time been a community, there were no houses and it looked bleak and empty. The Pilot Book assured me it was good holding ground in black, smelly mud, so I let the sails fall and sounded cautiously in to the shore to let go the anchor in seven metres.

With the wind in the north-west it was unusually cold for midsummer, and I tackled the ritual of lighting the cabin stove, a charcoal-burning beast as temperamental as a prima donna. A friend of mine had one in his boat and said it warmed him twice, once with the effort of lighting it and again when he eventually got it going. Actually it was easier to get instant warmth when both burners of the galley stove were roaring away, but it was heavy on paraffin and could soon become life-threatening if the cabin doors were tightly shut. I longed for the coal-burning bogey stove I had on a steel ketch I once owned. It would burn driftwood as well and kept the cabin warm and cosy, while wet clothes could be dried overnight. I was incensed when the insurers insisted it should be replaced with a diesel heater that, in comparison to the bogey stove, was useless.

Favoured by *Halcyon's* insurers because it was 'safe', the charcoal burner was equally hopeless at radiating heat, though it had one redeeming feature: it could boil a kettle balanced on the top of it, and I whiled away the morning drinking innumerable cups of coffee and eating digestive biscuits, jammed up close to the stove reading the intriguing life story of Alistair Cooke, whose brilliant 'Letter from America' on BBC Radio I had listened to avidly for years.

During the afternoon occasional wind squalls hurtled down from the hills and churned the surface of the loch into white froth, and when *Halcyon* heeled over slightly I was glad I had taken the skipper's advice and let out plenty of anchor chain. The cold wind put paid to any thoughts of inflating the dinghy and going ashore, and failing to get a good radio signal to listen to the BBC shipping forecast ahead of the six o'clock news, I turned my attention to preparing the 'cuddies', and fried them in olive oil along with sauté potatoes and canned butter beans. They were delicious, and I drank the skipper's health with a glass of red wine.

The wind moaned through the rigging all night, and it was still cold and windy when I reluctantly climbed out of my warm sleeping bag at 8 a.m. and opened the hatch to investigate a mysterious noise. It sounded like the grunt of a seal, and when I opened the hatch I found I was right, except that instead of just one seal there seemed to be hundreds of them bobbing up and down in the water and completely surrounding *Halcyon*. There had been lots of seals when I anchored in Loch Eynort in South Uist, but nothing like this lot; it was if Dirascal was the site of an annual seal convention and I had chosen the wrong time to be there. As a peace offering I threw them the remains of the cuddies, but they sniffed at them disdainfully and sank with their snouts showing just above the surface. We must have stared at each other for several minutes until, frozen to the marrow, I retreated to the cabin for breakfast and a hot drink.

They were still there an hour later when I went on deck, and it was a creepy feeling knowing that a hundred eyes were silently watching my every move while I hoisted the sails and lifted the anchor ready to depart for Loch Tealasavay. When the sails filled and *Halcyon* surged ahead, they moved aside like columns of well-trained soldiers to let her through. It was uncanny. Sea creatures can be more community-orientated than humans, and there was such a large gathering I seriously wondered if I had inadvertently trespassed on a part of Loch Resort sacred to seals. I sailed away and left them in peace.

The weather dictated that my visit to Loch Tealasavay would be short and swift, so I saw little of it. It faces west and is open to the Atlantic, and when I cleared the mouth of Loch Resort and turned to starboard to pass between the island of Greine Sgeir and the rocky headland marking the entrance to Tealasavay, there was a horrible swell running. Inside the loch it was difficult to manoeuvre even under engine, and anchoring would have been impossible. Fortunately the entrance to Loch Tamanavay was close at hand, with a narrow entrance that opened out into a well-sheltered inner loch, and I motored to a deep inlet at the head called Loch Cheann Chuisil and sounded towards the shore as close as I dared, letting go the anchor in five metres.

The head of the loch gave way to a narrow glen that threaded between two ranges of high hills, and I was concerned it could be a perfect funnel for wind to blast through. With the skipper's warning in mind I let go plenty of extra chain, but in fact it was a delightful anchorage, out of the wind and far enough away from the open sea to escape the swell.

The sky was dark and threatened rain, though it was a lot warmer than in Loch Resort and I enjoyed a sandwich lunch in the cockpit. Hoping the weather might be fair enough for me to get a walk on the hills the next day, I spread out the Ordnance Survey map and was overjoyed to discover that Mealisval, the highest mountain in Lewis, 574 metres, was at the far end of the glen, and I worked out a route that would take me to the summit. The one big snag was that it would be a round walk of ten miles over rough country, plus the ascent of the mountain, but I knew that if I started early enough I could achieve it comfortably within the day. Still unable to get the weather forecast on either the BBC or Stornoway Coastguard frequencies, I hoped for the best and inflated the dinghy to have it ready for the morning.

It was a quiet night that bode well for the day, and I got up at 7 a.m. to pack my rucksack with a flask, sandwiches and waterproofs and, as an afterthought, included a small hand-held VHF radio, hoping that reception might be good enough on the top of the mountain to get a Coastguard weather forecast. There was no point in taking my digital camera. The battery charger had developed a fault while I was in Loch Leosavay, and both my batteries were flat. I always carried lots of emergency spares for the boat when cruising in the Hebrides, but never considered that the camera battery charger would give any trouble.

Although a thin mist was hanging low over the glen, it was dry and surprisingly warm when I rowed ashore and carried the dinghy above the high-water mark. The midges found me as soon as I stepped ashore, and though my midge repellent had been used up in Loch Leosavay I had come prepared with a more potent midge chaser, a small bottle of paraffin. Dabbed on my neck, face and arms it was revolting, but the midges thought so too and that was the object of the exercise. It was worth smelling like a barge engineer's overalls to be rid of the most fiendish little brutes that nature ever created.

According to the map, the glen at the head of the loch was called Glen Taman-isdale, and the mountain scenery was fantastic. A stalker's path climbed diagonally across the lower slopes of a steep hill for three miles until it reached the highest point of a rocky pass, before descending to remote Loch Raonasgall, on the floor of another glen the Ordnance Survey had not got a name for but which was incredibly steep-sided and the home of several pairs of ravens and a solitary buzzard.

The mist obligingly cleared away and revealed the east side of Mealisval hung with massive precipices, and I had to skirt round the bog-ridden base of its neighbour – with the tongue-twisting name of Mula Mac Sgiathain – and approach Mealisval from the west. It was a tough, exhausting climb up a demanding slope of thick deer grass, leading towards a gap between Mealisval and Mula Mac Sgiathain, and I was soon soaked in sweat. There were compensations, though. The east side of Mealisval that towered above the glen had been steep, desolate and uninviting; but the west side was a complete contrast with the shrill chirping of skylarks filling the air and the hillside scattered with wild flowers.

As I climbed higher, the grass gave way to a mass of boulders that provided an energetic scramble to the summit, but it was deeply disappointing to arrive just in time to see the view swallowed up by a bank of cloud, which appeared from nowhere and sat stubbornly on the summit cairn as though some petulant weather god was determined to deprive me of my reward. Visibility was only a few metres and the north-west wind bitterly cold.

Sheltering behind a rock, I pulled on my anorak, poured a mug of coffee from the flask and switched on the VHF radio to wait for Stornoway Coastguard's 1310-hours weather bulletin. It came through loud and clear, and a female voice with a lilting Lewis accent cheered me with the information that the low had moved into the North Sea, and for the next few days the weather in the Hebrides would be breezy but fine and dry.

Half an hour later when, stiff-legged and cold, I could see it was obvious the spiteful weather god had no intention of doing the decent thing and moving his cloud away, I gave up waiting and was retracing my steps carefully down the boulder field when above me the sun suddenly burst through and revealed the peaked summit in all its glory. The cloud rapidly lifted and uncovered a remarkable panorama of the Atlantic and a superb bird's-eye view of Uig Bay, Gallan Head, the Flannan Isles and Loch Roag to the north, and the islands of Mealista and Scarp to the south. It was a missed photo opportunity I deeply regretted, and I have since made a point of carrying on board an 'old-fashioned' camera with a colour film in it.

The descent down the hillside and the long walk back through the glens could best be described as a muscle-aching plod, eased only with a glass of good whisky when I was back aboard *Halcyon*, though when I climbed onto my bunk I felt a great sense of achievement. Bad weather had thwarted my ascent of the highest hill in Harris, but the ascent of the highest hill in Lewis, the views of the wide seascape of the grey Atlantic and the astounding jagged coastline would linger long in my memory.

The Coastguard's promised breeze was blowing from the north-west when I left Loch Tamanavay under engine the following morning, though I was not aware of it until I cleared the entrance and could see surf breaking on yet another island with the name of Duisker, this one off the northern tip of Scarp. My wind gauge was wavering between ten and twelve knots, the bottom end of force four, and a steep, breaking swell heading into the entrance of the Sound between Scarp and Harris reinforced the fishing boat skipper's warning to keep away from it when the wind was from the north. I was going to sail round the west side of Scarp, by way of a narrow passage between the island and Duisker, and then keeping well to seaward to clear an evil patch called Obe Rocks and two submerged rocks identified by breaking seas on the south side of Scarp. Once that had been safely negotiated, I had a course prepared to lead me between Old Rocks and Huisinis Glorigs to the wide entrance of West Loch Tarbert and Leosavay.

Normally I would have felt exhilarated at the prospect of a challenging sail, but instead I felt hugely depressed. With the weather being so uncertain I had reluctantly accepted that any possibility of sailing to St Kilda had now faded, and I had made up my mind to return to Loch Leosavay. It was about fifteen miles, and the way the swell was crashing into the cliffs of Scarp and leaping high into the air, I could see I was in for a spirited sail, and clipped my safety line onto a ring in the cockpit. Not keen to battle with the big gaff mainsail and heavy boom, I made life a lot easier for myself by hoisting only the mizzen and jib and keeping the engine running until I was well into the open sea past Duisker and a nearby group of submerged rocks.

The swell seemed abnormally high for such a light wind, and I was glad that wind and tide were running in the same direction. Switching off the engine, I steered due west, and each time *Halcyon* was lifted high by a wave I could vaguely glimpse the lonely sea-lashed island of Gasker, five miles ahead in the Atlantic. It was noted for its seal colony, though little else.

Ignoring the swell and carefully avoiding colliding with *Halcyon*, a flock of gannets streaked out of the sky to furiously dive-bomb a shoal of fish I must have been sailing over. Almost touching the sides of the hull and plunging below the bowsprit, these dazzling birds, with their yellow heads and long spiky wings, dived with aerodynamic perfection onto the unsuspecting fish and surfaced a few minutes later to shake the water off their backs and soar into the air again, only to repeat the dive a few metres away. It was awe-inspiring to be so close to such an amazing sight and I was a long way beyond my plotted turning point before the birds had eaten their fill and moved away.

Having to gybe round to port to regain my course was unnerving in the heavy swell, and there was a horrible crash of pans and plates falling out of the galley when a playful sea pitched *Halcyon* into a trough, but the ordeal was soon over and I sailed along the south side of Scarp about a mile offshore, keeping a wary eye on the terrifying cauldron of breaking seas that concealed the Old Rocks.

The wind became fitful and gusty in the lee of the island, and *Halcyon* rolled heavily in the swell, causing the gaff of the standing lugsail on the mizzen to slam violently against the mast, and before I could do anything the halyard had chafed through and parted, and with a rush the sail came down and crashed into the cockpit, covering me in a cocoon of canvas and rope and knocking me away from the tiller. All I could think of was that the dangerous Old Rocks were less than a mile ahead, and with all my strength I fought to heave the canvas off my head and fling it onto the after deck.

The jib was flogging madly, and I could see that *Halcyon* had rounded up into the wind and was being tossed about like a cork. Seas were breaking over the side deck and flooding the cockpit; but, scared that the broken halyard might have gone over the side and round the propeller, I dared not start the engine. Hastily cranking the winch of the roller-reefing gear, I wound the jib out of harm's way; then I remembered that before leaving the Clyde I had rigged a spare halyard on the mizzen mast to enable me to lift the outboard motor in and out of the dinghy on my own.

I had spliced a large karabiner on the end and it took only minutes to clip it onto the gaff, hoist the sail, run the jib out, then hurl the damaged halyard into a locker out of harm's way, and order was restored. The icy water slopping around in the cockpit quickly drained away, and once clear of Scarp the sails began to draw again. A little over two hours later, with all the horror of broken halyards, roaring waves, submerged rocks and flooded cockpits left behind, *Halcyon* was anchored once more in Loch Leosavay in sight of Amhuinnsuidhe Castle and I was changed into dry clothes, drinking a mug of coffee laced with a generous dash of whisky and stirring a pan of corned beef hash on the stove. The first leg of the return to the Minch was safely behind me.

9

LEVERBURGH – THE COUNTESS'S BIRTH CONTROL – THE SCARP MIRACLE

One of several Gaelic words for an isolated rock is Bo, and there is a sprinkling of them in the Sound of Taransay. Some have their heads above water and others lurk below it, and when I left Leosavay the following morning bound for the Sound of Harris I was astonished to see a clinker-built dinghy perched on the top of Bo Usbig. Wondering if it might be a stranded angler, I edged alongside as close as I dared and could faintly make out the name Saint Brendan on the transom, but there was no one on board and it was in a very poor state, full of holes and obviously a derelict. Having lain abandoned for years on a distant shore, it had most likely been lifted off by a high tide, and following the coracles of other Irish saints, had drifted across the ocean until it fetched up on holy Taransay.

The fresh wind that had given me a sparkling sail down from Scarp the previous day had fallen away to a light breeze, though the sea was still feeling the influence of the vigorous low that had crossed the top of Scotland. Off Toe Head there was a lofty swell and I could appreciate why some of the old fishermen I had sailed with called it Cape Difficulty. I stayed well offshore until I could get a bearing on the island of Coppay. Like Gasker, its lonely neighbour, the little island of Coppay has no admirers among romantic novelists and poets, though for centuries many a sailor has been very glad to see it. It positively identifies the north-west entrance to the Sound of Harris, and in the lee of Toe Head the seas mercifully died down and I was able to slurp a small bottle of orange juice and nibble a piece of flapjack.

Longing for fresh vegetables, sausages, eggs and bacon, I had opted to give the Cope Channel a miss and go through the rocks and islands on the north side of the

Sound to call at Leverburgh, where I knew there was a shop. First, though, I had six miles of uncluttered sea to enjoy before I would have to take down the sails and use the engine, and to help me on my way a weak sun smiled from behind the clouds and two pairs of porpoise surged ahead in front of the bowsprit. Helped by a fast-flowing tide, the six miles went by very quickly, and at a red buoy marking the western end of Stromay Channel that led to the Leverburgh Channel I stowed the sails, started the engine and, mindful of the awkward passage ahead, took a deep breath.

For what seemed an eternity I strove to identify beacons as I shot by them, and to maintain the correct course in tortuous channels while keeping keep clear of submerged reefs and fighting the strong cross-tides, eventually reaching Leverburgh only to find that all space on the pier was taken by fishing boats. Anchoring off a wide concrete slip, I rowed ashore and set off on the long trek to the shop carrying a large rucksack.

Leverburgh had a forlorn, neglected look about it. Originally called An t-Ob after a nearby loch, the community was renamed Leverburgh as a mark of respect to, or perhaps more likely on the instructions of, Lord Leverhulme, the English business tycoon who made his fortune manufacturing soap, and ploughed enormous sums of money into Harris when he became the proprietor in 1919. His dream was to transform Leverburgh from an almost forgotten island community into a major fishing port, and he built new roads and jetties, kippering sheds, new houses for the locals and even a fleet of trawlers.

It was a boom town, and a major employer that attracted workers from all over the Hebrides, though when Leverhulme died in 1925 his family, horrified at the amount of money it was costing, pulled the rug from under the scheme and the enterprise slid rapidly into decline. It seemed to me that Leverburgh was a sleeping tiger that had tremendous potential, though the whole place, not least the harbour, was desperately in need of an injection of cash. Alas, however, there would never be another Lord Leverhulme.

Despite the shortcomings of the village, the local shop was exceptionally well stocked, even with batteries that would fit my camera; and, bent under a heavy load, I trudged the mile or so back to the slip and rowed out to *Halcyon*. While waiting for the coffee pot to boil, I used the time to shin up the mizzen mast and fit a new mizzen halyard into place. The chart showed a straightforward if somewhat winding route back into the Sound, which was made easier by following in the wake of a lobster boat whose friendly skipper said he was heading for the Sound on his way to Berneray, and would show me the way.

With the tide under me and all sails hoisted, I enjoyed a very pleasant run to Loch Rodel, and bathed in sunlight it was a very different place to the one I had left the previous week. I was sad to leave the Atlantic side of the Hebrides, but the east side of Harris and Lewis had its own magnetism and there was much to see.

With the tide on the ebb, I had to wait several hours at anchor in the loch before there was sufficient water over a shingle bar in the narrow channel leading to Rodel Harbour and the unusual anchorage of Poll an Tigh-Mhail, but the strength of the hidden moon eventually pulled the tide back in again, and I pointed *Halcyon* at the entrance.

The neat little harbour with stone jetties dried out at low water, but close to it the sculpting forces of ancient glaciers had gouged out a handy pool, reasonably protected by three little islands, and the Western Isles Council had added the finishing touch by laying a few visitors' moorings.

I picked one up in the lee of Vallay, the largest of the three islands, and it was nice to know that for a change *Halcyon* was secured to a large lump of concrete, instead of worrying whether the anchor was well dug in or just hanging onto a clump of seaweed. There was a hotel above the old harbour, and with an appetite sharpened by the run from Leverburgh I inflated the dinghy and went ashore to sample the lunch menu.

I was hoping for local seafood, but if I had asked the laconic gent behind the bar for truffles and champagne or just a bowl of soup the answer would have been the same. 'There is only sandwiches. You can have cheese, ham and pickle, or tuna and mayonnaise.' Not to put too much of a strain on the kitchen facilities, I settled for plain cheese, and sat twiddling my thumbs in the empty bar for half an hour before even they arrived.

Leaving the depressing hotel, I felt in need of something to lift my spirits, and it came in a most unexpected way. Above the harbour I wandered into the ancient square-towered Church of St Clement, and was surprised that it had neither pews nor altar and was completely empty. An information leaflet informed me that St Clement was the patron saint of boatmen and fishermen, and that the church was first mentioned in 1549.

The early MacLeod chiefs of Dunvegan on Skye, who also owned Harris, had probably built it, and the church was their burial place. One of the chiefs buried in the church was Alexander Crotach, who was a hunchback due to a sword wound that severed the muscles in his neck during the Battle of Bloody Bay, near Tobermory, in 1480.

The church had fallen into disrepair, but had been restored in 1873 by Catherine, Countess of Dunmore, whose husband's father, the 5th Earl of Dunmore, had bought Harris from the MacLeods in 1834. (It was Catherine's son who had built Amhuinnsuidhe Castle.) The church tracts were full of the usual historical stuff, but when I went outside to photograph the church tower I learnt a lot more interesting facts about the Church of St Clement than the leaflet had dared to reveal.

A minibus arrived full of elderly men and women on a guided tour and, having delivered his spiel about the MacLeod chiefs and who occupied the tombs along the inside of the church, the guide went on to tell how the church had been restored thanks to the benevolence of the Countess of Dunmore. 'But,' he said, raising his voice to command attention, 'high up on the outside of the tower there was a naked male statue, and his masculine bit was standing out bold, like. And d'ye know what?'

He paused, but the group looked blank except for a large lady who said irritably, 'What?'

'Well,' continued the guide. 'The Countess being Victorian and prude, like, was offended by this statue's masculine bit being on show, and ordered one of her gamekeepers to bring his gun and shoot it off.'

The audience gasped with horror. 'Yep,' said the guide, 'The gamekeeper took aim and bang! – one offending willy disappeared in a cloud of dust.' Some of the ladies giggled with embarrassment, but the large lady was not amused.

'What a load of rubbish!' she stormed. 'I thought we were on this tour to learn historical facts.'

'But it is a fact,' protested the guide. 'It's documented in a local history book.'

The large lady snorted angrily, but a quiet, balding man in a kilt, who appeared to be the large lady's husband, bravely spoke up in the guide's defence.

'I'm afraid he's right, Effie my dear,' he said. 'I've got the book here and, apart from that story, it tells of a man from Berneray who married his third wife, aged sixteen, when he was seventy- five; they had nine children and he was ninety when he died. As a gynaecologist I find that fascinating.'

The large lady glared at him. 'Yes, you would!' she snarled. 'Nine children – the man was an animal. The poor lassie must have been worn out. You men have only one thing on your mind. If ever a man deserved the Countess of Dunmore's form of birth control it was him!'

The other ladies nodded their heads and muttered their approval and, sensing the situation could get out of control, the guide quickly ushered the group into the church with the promise that the interior was well worth a visit. Meeting the minibus party was the perfect antidote to the disappointment of the hotel, and I returned to the harbour still laughing at the story.

Chris Merlin, a friend who owned the post office when I lived in the village of Ravenglass on the Cumbrian coast, had moved to live on Harris with his Belgian wife Annick, so before returning to *Halcyon*, I phoned the number he had given me and was delighted to find that they lived on the edge of Loch Finsbay, about three miles up the coast from Rodel. 'You won't be able to get out of Rodel until at least half-tide tomorrow,' said Chris, 'but it'll be great to see you. Come and have a meal with us. Loch Finsbay is easy to get into and it's a good anchorage.'

Stornoway Coastguard's evening forecast on VHF promised that the wind would continue to be light and, true to their word, when I woke it was calm and the sun was warming the deck. Obeying the Pilot Book's instruction to wait until

'Happy Hour' at Loch Finsbay. Chris Merlin and Annike on the left

the stone base of a perch marking the channel was submerged and the depth would be three metres, it was early afternoon before I was able to nudge *Halcyon* carefully out of the haven into Loch Rodel and make the short run to Loch Finsbay. The entrance was easily identified between two small islands, though it was a sketch map in the Imray Pilot Book that was the key to avoiding sunken rocks along a zigzag course that led into the upper loch, and I dropped anchor close to where a fine old wooden yacht that had seen better days was swinging idly on a mooring.

I spent three days enjoying the generous hospitality of the Merlins, eating and drinking too much and meeting their fisherman neighbours who worked creels along the coast. Known as the Bays District, it was a fascinating corner of Harris that had seen hard times, and the forlorn ruins of croft houses were a reminder of the barbarous suffering inflicted on defenceless crofters and their families when, during the dreadful Clearances of the 19th century, they were driven from their homes in thousands and herded onto ships to be dumped in countries across the world.

Islanders have long memories and Donald Angus, my erstwhile shipmate, was from the Bays District and had an inborn hatred of lairds and landowners. Listening to his incredible story handed down through his family about an ancestor, Ruairidh Mhor, Big Rory, I could understand why.

A leading landowner on Skye, Sir Alexander MacDonald of Sleat and his brother-in-law Norman MacLeod, of Harris, devised a monstrous plan to make money by abducting the wives and children of crofters in South Harris and transporting them to America to be sold as slaves. They chartered a ship called the *William* and, choosing a day when they knew the men would be away gathering sheep, they sailed it into Loch Finsbay, where a pressgang went ashore and forced the women and children out of their homes and onto the ship.

The men were grief-stricken when they discovered what had happened, but were no match for a bunch of armed thugs, and none of them dared attempt a rescue. But Big Ruairidh, a man renowned for his strength, rowed out to the ship during the night and, while the sailors were asleep, he opened the hatch to the hold and lifted his wife out. The others were less fortunate and the next day the ship sailed for America.

The heart-breaking story might have ended there had the captain not put into Donaghadee in Northern Ireland for repairs, and some of the women escaped and raised the alarm. The authorities arrested the crew and the women and children were freed. The incident caused a major scandal, but the establishment protected landed gentry like MacDonald and MacLeod and no action was taken against them.

It is easy to be drawn into the carefree way of life of the islands, and I felt I could have stayed for ever in lovely Loch Finsbay and the company of Chris and Annick; but the weather forecasts warned of unsettled weather ahead and, anxious to be on my way, I reluctantly said my goodbyes and put to sea under full sail with a friendly south-easterly pushing me northwards.

South Harris would have been just another solitary island, perhaps with a different name, had not the retreating glaciers that sculpted the Hebrides left a convenient strip of land the Gaels called Tairbeart (a narrow isthmus) that connected it to North Harris. It formed a natural barrier separating West Loch Tarbert on the Atlantic Ocean side from East Loch Tarbert on the Minch side, and the Vikings found it an ideal place to drag their boats across from one sea to the other.

Most yachts cruising the Minch side of South Harris are drawn to the island of Scalpay that dominates the entrance to East Loch Tarbert, mainly for the facilities it offers in two well-protected harbours, but also because the township of Tarbert that grew from the Viking settlement is another four miles down the loch and not very yacht-friendly. The needs of MacBrayne's car ferry take priority; there are no visitors' moorings and anchoring is very restricted. When I reached East Loch Tarbert after a very enjoyable sail from Finsbay, it was tempting to turn into the haven of Scalpay's north harbour, but I had another goal in mind.

Not very far away, and towering out of the sea with all the grandeur of its neighbours on Skye, was Clisham, 799 metres, the highest mountain on Harris and in the Hebrides. Bad weather had prevented me from climbing it when I was in West Loch Tarbert, but the barometer was steady and I was confident the weather would hold for a few days. The snag was that Clisham was on the west side of Harris and four miles by bus from Tarbert, and to be able to use the bus I needed a mooring close to the town. The Pilot Book was very pessimistic about my chances of finding one but, hoping something would turn up, I lowered the sails, started the engine, and headed for Tarbert in the wake of MacBrayne's car ferry arriving from Skye.

Beyond the ferry terminal there were plenty of moorings, but they all had small fishing boats attached to them, and after making several circuits without success I was about to admit defeat and turn for Scalpay when a man working on a boat I had passed a couple of times shouted, 'Are you looking for a mooring?'

'Yes,' I shouted back.

'How long will you be staying?'

'A couple of nights if I can. I'm hoping to climb Clisham and I need to catch the bus tomorrow morning.'

'Well, if that's all you want it for you can use mine. I'm just about to go across to dry out on the slip to get my engine fixed and I'll be there about three days.'

I manoeuvred *Halcyon* alongside and offered to pay him, but he refused. Slipping the mooring, he shouted, 'Just make sure you're off it by the time I come back,' and giving the engine full power he roared away.

Hardly able to believe my luck, I secured the mooring rope on *Halcyon's* fore deck and went below to sort through my stock of food to prepare a celebratory dinner. I settled on tinned steak, new potatoes and mushy peas.

The following morning I was on the 9.30 a.m. Tarbert to Stornoway bus as it drove from East Loch Tarbert, on the Minch side, across the narrow isthmus and hugged the edge of West Loch Tarbert, on the Atlantic side, before turning inland and contouring steeply and very conveniently across the eastern flanks of Clisham to give me a good start up the mountain.

Unhindered by clouds, the sun shone down from a bright blue sky and the whole mountainside shimmered in the heat. It was one of those days that confirmed the Hebrides as one of the most beautiful places in the world, and which the Western Isles Tourist Board went into raptures about, but due to the inconsistent weather pattern of the islands could more often be as rare as haggis and chips on the menu of a Hyde Park hotel. I had been very fortunate to see so little rain on my journey; a girl I knew who worked in a hotel in Stornoway went to clean a room after two English guests had departed, and found a very disgruntled note pinned to a pillow:

Thirty days we stayed in the Western Isles
And one day the sun was powerful
But it rained and blew for twenty-nine
Your weather is bloody awful.

Next year we're going to Tenerife
Where the sun is warm and browning
We might be ill from too much heat
But we'll walk without fear of drowning.

The steep grassy slopes gave way to broken rock as I climbed higher and the views were fantastic. They were even better from the summit cairn, where there was an endless panorama of rugged mountain peaks and ridges rippling away into the distance. I could clearly see Taransay to the south, and far out to the west I could vaguely make out the St Kilda islands and wished I had brought my binoculars.

I was busy taking photographs when a cheerful group of women in their twenties, all carrying rucksacks, suddenly appeared on the summit and flopped down on the rocks, gasping with relief. 'Would you like a drink?' shouted one sun-tanned beauty in shorts and a revealing T-shirt, brandishing a can of Coke towards me. 'I've got some more in my bag.' It was slightly warm, but at least it was wet and very welcome.

They said they were police cadets from Glasgow and were on a hill-walking holiday together to get fit. 'I wish I'd got fit before we started,' groaned one girl, who had a physique that would certainly have subdued a Glasgow hooligan misbehaving outside a pub on a Saturday night, but was rather a lot to carry up a mountain. Taking off a boot and sock, she revealed a nasty blister on her heel.

I helped with first aid to the blister and a sticking plaster, and was assured that my case would be considered with the utmost clemency should I ever commit a crime in Glasgow. They basked in the sun until the popularity of the leader of the party plunged to zero when she announced it was time to press on for the next summit. I was handed several cameras to take photographs of the group; then, bursting into song and with lots of waving, they marched off out of sight. The summit felt lonely without them.

It was a perfect day for hill walking and, loath to give it up, I was happily striding along the next ridge when I realised that I might miss the last bus on its return trip from Stornoway. Half running, half sliding down the hillside, I reached the road and was waiting for the bus when a van stopped and the driver asked if I would like a lift.

Not sure whether the bus had gone by or not, I thanked him and climbed in. A typical islander, he was curious to know everything about me and, when I mentioned I was cruising the Hebrides in a boat and was collecting interesting stories like the attempt to send mail across to Scarp with a rocket, he snorted angrily and said, 'Och, I can tell you a better story about Scarp that's much more interesting than trying to send letters in a rocket. It's about real islanders.'

He said his father had been born on Scarp and often talked about the time he was a young boy. His family were huddled round the peat fire in their home one cold night in January 1934 when word reached his mother that a crofter's wife on the island had given birth to a baby.

The next day it was obvious the mother was ill and needed a doctor, and one of the islanders rowed across to Huisinis on Harris to telephone for help. But the only telephone was out of order, so the postman's son biked it to the doctor's house in Tarbert sixteen miles away. The doctor raced to Huisinis in his car and was ferried across to Scarp, but said there was nothing he could do and the mother must be taken to hospital in Stornoway.

She had to endure a terrifying mile-long journey across the Sound, in rough seas, strapped to a wooden stretcher that was laid across an open rowing boat; and if that was not enough, she was then bounced along the sixteen gruelling miles to Tarbert on the floor of the local bus. But her ordeal was by no means over!

She was transferred to a car, and for nearly forty miles it swayed and lurched over a road that in the 1930s was a narrow, winding switchback of hills, bumps, bends and potholes. But she survived and reached Stornoway hospital, where to the surprise of everyone, not least the mother, she gave birth to another child.

'Island women were tough in those days,' chortled the driver. 'What a scoop it would have made for the television and the Guinness Book of Records. The twins were born on different days, on different islands and in different counties. How's that for a story of island life?'

He dropped me by the harbour in Tarbert and as he drove away he called out,

'Enjoy your sailing trip. Have a look at Loch Seaforth, it's the finest loch in the islands.'

10

TROLLS IN LOCH SEAFORTH – IS IT
LEWIS OR HARRIS? – THE BRAHAN SEER

My experience of sailing in Hebridean waters is that when the weather starts to become unsettled, the Coastguard marine forecasts tend to be more dependable than those dispensed by the cheerful ladies on BBC Radio Scotland; and, as there was nothing too alarming in Stornoway Coastguard's three-day forecast, it was a chance to give my usual pilgrimage to the Scalpay harbours a miss and take up the van driver's advice to 'have a look at Loch Seaforth'.

The entrance to the loch was only about three miles from Scalpay, and the quickest way from Tarbert was through a Sound on the north side of the island but, since my last visit, a bridge had been built between Scalpay and Harris and my chart was not up to date. Rather than risk decapitating *Halcyon*'s main mast, I chose to take the long way round, and on an overcast but dry morning, with a lively breeze from the west, I let go the mooring with a silent thanks to the kindly fisherman and pointed the bow towards the open sea.

When a storm in the winter of 1782 wreaked havoc among the fleets of ships plying the waters around Scotland, the Parliament in London was besieged with demands for lighthouses to be built and it led to the 'Act for Erecting Certain Lighthouses in the Northern Parts of Great Britain' and the founding of the Northern Lighthouse Board.

The site chosen for the first, and for a long time the only, lighthouse in the Hebrides, was on Eilean Glas (the grey island), a little headland jutting out from the east side of the Island of Scalpay, and when *Halcyon* cleared East Loch Tarbert and butted into the short swell of the Minch, I gybed round and steered for its tall

Eilean Glas lighthouse, Scalpay

white tower, painted with two distinctive red bands. It was only four miles from Eilean Glas to the entrance of Loch Seaforth, but it was hard work. Blanketed by the hills on the Harris coast, the fresh westerly breeze that had carried *Halcyon* down East Loch Tarbert was exasperatingly fluky and, irritated by uncontrolled gybes and the lifeless sails crashing from side to side in the swell, I lashed the lot down and started the engine.

Loch Seaforth forms part of the boundary line between Harris on the west side and Lewis on the east and any homesick Norwegian would feel at home there. It is a typical fjord almost twelve miles long, with deep water and towering mountains on either side, and appears to be inhabited by spiteful Trolls who resent strangers in boats intruding into their mountain kingdom. The first six mile stretch of the loch runs from south-east to north-west and is divided at its head by the mile-long expanse of Seaforth Island. For the next three miles it turns north-east until Upper Loch Seaforth forms a T-junction at its head.

Alas, entering what would otherwise have been a perfect anchorage in the upper loch is tantalisingly denied to most yachts by a shallow, rock-strewn rapid with a seven-knot tide race called The Narrows. If the Trolls are in a belligerent mood, they can drum up vicious winds and make anchoring elsewhere in the loch decidedly unpleasant; and my first clash with them was in Loch Maaruig, an anchorage on the west side of the loch about two and a half miles in from the sea.

They must have been watching as I cautiously steered *Halcyon* past submerged rocks towards the collection of houses on the shore, and waited until I had dropped anchor. The wind had been westerly and the anchorage sheltered from it, but with fiendish glee the little monsters swung it completely round to the east, compressed it between two mountain tops and catapulted it like a tornado at Loch Maaruig. I was below making coffee and sandwiches when, with a roar like an express train, the wind appeared from nowhere, bowling *Halcyon* over onto her side, sending the kettle flying off the cooker and me crashing onto the cabin floor, together with a horrible mixture of milk, coffee, sugar, bread, margarine, corned beef and Branston pickle.

Scrambling into the cockpit, it was if a hurricane had struck. The calm surface of the loch was now a boiling mass of wind-lashed waves that sent spray flying mast high when they crashed with a sickening thud against the hull; but, more serious, the anchor was dragging and *Halcyon* was drifting stern first towards the shore. I had to get out of there, and fast. Starting the engine, I ran forward to crank the anchor winch, but the chain was like a solid bar of steel and I had to keep surging *Halcyon* ahead under power then rushing to the winch and cranking furiously to take up the slack before the chain became taut again.

By the time the anchor was safely against the stem head roller I was utterly exhausted, but there was no time to lose. Somewhere between me and safety were submerged rocks and, blinded by spray and buffeted by the fierce wind, it was with more good luck than judgement that I managed to avoid hitting them and escape into the deep water of Loch Seaforth. The Trolls must have hooted with delight that their lark had chased me out of the anchorage and, enjoying their cat and mouse game, they had more to come.

Keeping in the lee of the eastern shore, I had worked my way up as far as Seaforth Island when the strong easterly wind died away as quickly as it came and was replaced by a light northerly. Sheltered from the wind and only a mile away was a jetty in front of a shooting lodge that the Pilot Book recommended as a good anchorage. Cold, hungry and very tired I sounded in to eight metres and let go the anchor.

It was just what the Trolls wanted me to do! I had cleaned up the mess below, enjoyed a warming coffee with a dram of nerve-soothing whisky and prepared potatoes and a tin of steak for my evening meal. I had even lit the charcoal-burning cabin stove to combat the chilly air, and was tidying up on deck when I happened to glance down the loch and was shocked to see a black squall racing towards me.

With evil delight, the Trolls had again spun the wind round 180 degrees, and before I regained the cockpit a screeching wind slammed into *Halcyon* and there was a tremendous crash in the cabin as pans and crockery were flung from the galley when she heeled over. I clung on to a grab rail waiting for the squall to pass over, but when I saw that the jetty and the shore appeared to be rushing towards me I realised that the anchor was again dragging and rushed to start the engine and raise it. But the Trolls had anticipated this and each time I tried to crank the winch they fired off another violent squall that swung *Halcyon* broadside to the wind, driving her ever closer to the rocky shore.

In desperation I gave the engine full throttle and steered into deep water close to Seaforth Island, with nearly thirty metres of chain and the anchor dangling from the bow, and how the Trolls relished adding to my misery. While straining every muscle to crank in the heavy chain, I was bombarded with merciless gusts that spun *Halcyon* round like a piece of driftwood and knocked me off my feet or drenched me with spray. I was completely worn out; and when the last link of the chain slid down the hawse pipe and the anchor clanged against the stem head, my only thought was to find shelter.

With the squalls now from the south, the obvious choice was the northern tip of Seaforth Island where it rose steeply above the loch. Though, at ten metres, the depth was more than I was happy about, it was wonderfully protected and I let go the anchor, but this time I ran out the full length of my fifty-metre chain. The Trolls were furious, and huffed and puffed for an hour bouncing nasty squalls off the mountain sides from all directions, but the anchor held and, tired of their game, they retreated to their lair to sulk and hurl the occasional half-hearted blast to spin *Halcyon* round on the end of the chain.

The cabin was a dreadful mess, but order was gradually restored and a hot meal did wonders for reviving morale. Hunched close by the stove, I spread the charts out on the table and planned my next move along the coast of Lewis. It was interesting to note that, in his *Yachtsman's Pilot*, Martin Lawrence warned that Loch Seaforth was subject to dangerous squalls from unexpected directions, yet he made no mention of the Trolls. Maybe he had not worked with Hebridean fishermen, whose lives were enormously influenced by superstition.

In ancient times, disputes about where the island of Harris became the island of Lewis and vice versa sparked off many a bloody feud between neighbouring clans, and it was only when the clan chiefs realised it was not going to be settled by tit-for-tat massacres that they agreed on a boundary line drawn between Loch Seaforth in the east and Loch Resort in the west, and running along several miles of exceedingly wild and wet terrain.

I once attended a lecture by a historian who sparked off a lively debate by declaring there were no such places as the Island of Lewis or the Island of Harris. His reasoning was that, since they were both on the same land mass, encircled by the sea, it should be called the Island of Lewis and Harris. He had no takers for his way of thinking and was booed out of the room.

Why the island was divided into two separate 'kingdoms', whose identities and independence are still hotly defended, is lost in the mists of time; but historians blame fratricidal skirmishing within the clan MacLeod, who ruled Lewis after the Vikings lost control of the Hebrides in the 13th century.

It was the same clan treachery and skulduggery that lost the MacLeods the control of Lewis and Harris to the MacKenzies of Kintail in 1610. Later granted the title Earl of Seaforth, after whom the loch was named, the MacKenzies were haunted by an alarming prophecy that the male line was doomed, made by

Kenneth MacKenzie – Coinneach Odhar (Con-yak-our), dun-coloured Kenneth – the Brahan Seer, a servant at Brahan Castle, the MacKenzies' seat near Inverness.

He was gifted with second sight, but made the mistake of being too honest in replying to a request from Isabella, wife of the 3rd Earl, to look into the magic stone that gave him his power and check on how her husband was behaving himself while he was away on a visit to Paris. It is strange that in his stone he did not see his own fate or he might have lied that he saw the Earl living in a monastery, praying three times a day and living on bread and cheese, but instead he unwisely told her that he saw him in a gilded room 'grandly decked out in velvets, with silks and cloth of gold, and on his knees before a fair lady, his arm round her waist, and her hand pressed to his lips'.

It was not what Isabella wanted to hear, and in a jealous fury she accused the Seer of slandering the good name of the Seaforths and condemned him to a grisly death by being dropped head-first into a barrel of burning tar. Coinneach Odhar's desperate pleas for mercy went unheard and, staring into his magic stone, he avenged the injustice with a curse, declaring, 'I see into the far future and I read the doom of the race of my oppressor. The long-descended line of Seaforth will, ere many generations have passed, end in extinction and sorrow.'

He went on to predict much hardship and unhappiness for the Seaforths, especially the last chief in the line, who would have four sons, all of whom would die before him.

'He may know his sons are doomed to death, that his broad lands shall pass away to the stranger, and that his race shall come to an end.'

With uncanny accuracy, the prophecy came true and, with no sons to follow him, the title became extinct when the last Earl died in 1815 and his estate passed to his eldest daughter. She sold the island to a relative, whose ill-conceived ideas only plunged him deeply into debt and, when he died, his widow joyfully unloaded the burden of the family estate by selling it in 1844 to Mr James Matheson, the MP for Ross and Cromarty. The MacKenzies, Earls of Seaforth, had held the island for over two centuries but, as the Brahan Seer had prophesied, the 'broad lands' passed into the hands of a stranger.

11

THE BLUE MEN OF THE MINCH – SAVED BY A GHOST – HMS *IOLAIRE*

The Lewis coastline between Loch Seaforth and Stornoway is wild and barren, with no roads or habitation for a large part of it; but to explore its many sea lochs by boat when the weather is settled and the restless Minch is in a kindly mood is an unforgettable joy. It truly is a cruising man's dreamland and, mercifully, its remoteness and unpredictable weather have protected it from being swamped by the ever-increasing fleets of mainland-based charter yachts.

On the negative side, large-scale charts are as rare as topless sunbathers, and tidal streams can sluice up and down the coast like a mill race, but a good *Yachtsman's Pilot* is the key that opens up the delights of at least ten sheltered sea lochs, each with their own special beauty.

When, on a bright and breezy morning, I happily shook the last drops of Loch Seaforth water off the anchor, sailed out into the Minch and set a course for the lighthouse on the headland of Rubh Uisenis, I had one of them in mind; Loch Sealg (Shell). First, though, I had to go through the Sound of Shiant that separates Lewis from the Shiant Isles, five miles offshore, and notorious for its strong tides and scary tidal overfalls. I had planned to be at the entrance to the Sound at slack water and be whizzed through on the flood, but it was soon clear from the white-topped seas breaking all around, and *Halcyon* being swept backwards, that the ebb was still running strongly. Eventually the overfalls died away and, once the tide had turned, we soared towards Rubh Uisensis lighthouse at eight knots.

It was a sobering experience. Although the sea was relatively quiet, many of the overfalls had slopped heavily on deck and into the cockpit. Not for nothing did the Sound of Shiant get its reputation, and I shuddered at the thought of what the conditions would be like when there was even a moderate wind against the tide.

Away to starboard, the uninhabited Shiant Isles (Shunt) shimmered on the water like a fairy kingdom and it was easy to appreciate why the Gaelic name, Na h-Eileanan Seunta, meant 'enchanted islands'. In all the years I had sailed in the Hebrides I had never landed on them and, as the weather was reasonably settled, I was sorely tempted, but I knew the anchorage to be very insecure and I dared not leave *Halcyon* while I went ashore.

Donald Angus always warned me to keep away from the Shiants. Highly superstitious, he was afraid of the islands because the last family to live on them had met a tragic end. He believed the islands were haunted by their ghosts and by an evil tribe of kelpies (water spirits) called the Blue Men of the Minch, who played nasty tricks on sailors and could cast a spell on a boat or even sink it. Donald Angus's warning conjured up worrying images of the sinister blue tribe shinning down the chain and lifting *Halcyon*'s anchor off the bottom and towing her out to sea, leaving me helplessly stranded ashore.

It was enough to convince me to keep away from the Shiants; the Trolls of Loch Seaforth had been ordeal enough! Rounding the headland of Rubh Uisensis I eased the sheets and, with a freshening wind filling the sails, pressed on for the sanctity of Loch Sealg.

Only four miles beyond the Sound of Shiant, the wide entrance to Loch Sealg is divided into two channels by the elongated expanse of Eilean Lubhard (Yoo-Urt) – Yew Tree Island, but the island blends so naturally into the shoreline it can be as difficult to identify as an oystercatcher's nest. By way of a channel on the south side there are sheltered anchorages to be found at the head of the loch, but the one I was most familiar with was the inlet of Tob Limervay, hidden away in Caolas a' Tuath (the North Passage).

With a post office still bravely clinging on to life, a telephone and a water tap, the extremely isolated crofting community provides some of the basic needs of cruising types, but the anchorage is open to southerly winds and, anxious as I was for a peaceful night, the sight of moored fishing boats by the village jetty pitching heavily in a swell was enough to make me plump for a little bay a mile away on the lee side of Eilean Lubhard. It was so small it was barely a wiggle on the chart, but I let go the anchor into what appeared to be an underwater forest of kelp, gave the chain a good tug and hoped for the best.

Weary from my ordeal in Loch Seaforth and the splash through the Sound of Shiant overfalls, and feeling chilled by a remarkably cold wind for the time of year, I had made a quick meal, swallowed a warming dram and fallen fast asleep on my bunk when the shrill sound of an alarm pierced my numbed brain. Struggling awake, I switched on the cabin lights and peered at the clock. It was 2.30 a.m., and above the chart table the depth sounder was bellowing for attention and warning that there was less than two metres under the keel.

I had no recollection of switching on the alarm and, more puzzling, the tide table was open on the chart table and showed that the tide had another hour to fall. I was mystified, but the message was clear. If I did not move *Halcyon*, her keel would soon be locked in an intimate embrace with the saw-toothed rocks that encircled Eilean Lubhard; and, starting the engine, I rushed to crank the anchor off the bottom.

It took only a few minutes to move into deeper water and drop anchor again, and I went back to my sleeping bag furious with myself for not checking the day's rise and fall of the tide more carefully. It was a weird experience. I had absolutely no recollection of setting the depth alarm or of leaving the tide table open and could only guess that, like round-the-world sailor Joshua Slocum's yacht *Spray*, which had been steered to safety through a gale by the spectre of the Pilot of one of Columbus's ships, the *Pinta*, *Halcyon* had been saved from disaster by the ghost of Dr John Jago, who was obviously still on board making sure that no fool wrecked his 'dream ship'. Probably a more plausible explanation was that my mind and body were sorely in need of uninterrupted sleep.

The sound of a brisk southerly whistling through the rigging woke me about 6 a.m., but, snug in the tiny bay, *Halcyon* was well protected with only an occasional gust spiralling her round the anchor chain. My disturbed night and the whistling wind gave me the perfect excuse to linger in the warm cocoon of my sleeping bag and admire the workmanship of John Jago's laminated deck beams above my head and the varnished lockers. Glancing around, I could only speculate on what the popular yacht designer Jack Laurent Giles had in mind when he designed *Halcyon*, but he had produced a safe cruising boat of great character, superbly suited to cruising the west of Scotland.

With a main cabin like the inside of Fingal's Cave, I enjoyed a standard of comfort few boats of the same length could offer and, thanks to the lifting centre plate, I was able to sneak into shallow anchorages keel boat owners could only dream about. But the plus point for me was *Halcyon*'s large chart table with stowage space for charts and shelves for books, and I pulled out the ship's copy of *The Scottish Islands* to see what it had to say about Eilean Lubhard.

This hefty tome, incredibly well researched and illustrated by architect and sailing man Hamish Haswell-Smith, is as indispensable as the pilot books and Reeds Almanac to anyone cruising in Scottish waters and, true to form, Eilean Lubhard was well documented. That five families had scratched a survival existence from the island's rock and bog in the 19th century would hardly merit a mention in a tourist brochure; but the fact that Bonnie Prince Charlie hid on it for four days in 1746 will doubtless one day catapult this little-known corner of Lewis into the glare of publicity and a place on the inevitable 'Bonnie Prince Charlie Trail'.

Before he sailed across from Benbecula to Skye disguised as Flora MacDonald's maid, the Prince had landed near the head of Loch Seaforth, and with guides set off to walk across the moors and hills to Stornoway, where his supporters had arranged for a ship to take him to France. But the party got lost during the night and eventually reached the edge of the town only to be told that, when the ship's captain discovered that his passenger was to be the Prince himself, he refused to sail.

A small boat was found and the Prince and his supporters attempted to sail across the Minch to the mainland, but the weather was against them and Royal Navy ships could be seen on patrol, so the boat landed in a bay on the south shore of Eilean Lubhard. Fortunate to have the unswerving loyalty of the islanders, who risked their necks to help him to escape, the Prince sheltered from heavy rain under a sail stretched across a 'low pitiful hut' and, soaking wet and miserable, he lived on a diet of fish; no doubt spending some time reflecting on where his plans had gone wrong.

Dragging myself out of the sleeping bag I made a lunch of sandwiches and coffee, then rowed ashore in the dinghy to see if I could identify the bay where the Prince had landed. Above the anchorage, I found the foundations of old croft houses overgrown by grass, where the five families might have lived; but on the north side of the island, being buffeted by the wind and struggling over rough ground was very heavy going, so, hanging about just long enough to photograph the crashing surf sculpting the steep cliffs in a wide inlet, which might well have been the Prince's landing place, I turned and was blown back to *Halcyon*.

There were several very inviting anchorages and places I wanted to stop at along the twelve miles of coast from Loch Sealg to Stornoway, but a warning on VHF from the Coastguard that the fresh breeze would increase to an easterly gale within the next forty-eight hours prompted a change of plan, and I drew a pencil line on the chart direct to Stornoway, with every intention of following it. While on Lewis I wanted to visit a few of my old haunts, and if I had to be storm-bound for a few days, then Stornoway was the place to be. A man tending a fish-farm cage from a small boat gave me a wave as I motored down Caolas a' Tuath, and apart from seabirds, an otter and two seals, he was the only sign of life I had seen since arriving.

Rounding the high nose of Srianach Point at the entrance to the Caol, I was surprised by the strength of the wind that had now backed to south-east, and the ugly sea it had kicked up. Though *Halcyon* frequently buried her bowsprit into a trough and swept the deck with green water that swooshed into the cockpit, she sailed very contentedly under mizzen and jib, and a little over an hour after leaving we had covered the seven miles to the entrance of Loch Erisort.

Ironically, Loch Erisort was one of the few lochs on the east side of Lewis that had an abundance of corners sheltered from an easterly wind, but I resisted the temptation to turn into it and steered on for Stornoway. With only three miles to go to the safety of the harbour, the wind suddenly backed to the east and increased to a rage, and the seas, as if not sure how to deal with it, reared up in a panic on all sides, throwing *Halcyon* about like a discarded toy.

I hurriedly dropped the mizzen, rolled two reefs in the jib and seemed to be making good progress but, as the harbour entrance got closer, it was soon clear that as well as moving forward *Halcyon* was being blown sideways towards the dreaded Beasts of Holm. This group of rocks on the east side of the harbour entrance caused a terrible loss of life when, in the early hours of New Year's Day 1919, HMS *Iolaire*, an elegant steam yacht requisitioned by the Admiralty, drove onto the rocks in bad weather and over two hundred servicemen returning from the 1914–18 war were lost.

Unlike the *Iolaire*, I had daylight on my side, and when I started the engine and the propeller gripped the water, the bow swung back on course, and I made for Arnish Point lighthouse and the outer harbour. The fishing fleet was also steaming in to avoid the gale, and when the boats thundered towards *Halcyon* at full speed with foaming bow waves, I fervently hoped that none of the skippers had been infuriated by a fool of a yachtsman who had read somewhere that power gives way to sail and had crossed the bow of one of the boats when it was trawling. But they gave me a friendly wave as they swept by, and leaving them to jostle for position in the fish dock I manoeuvred *Halcyon* alongside a vacant pontoon in an area reserved for pleasure craft.

Only a step ahead of the gale I had arrived at Stjarna (Anchor Bay), Stron a Bhaigh (Nose of the Bay), and perhaps the most appropriate of the three, Portrona (Port of Seals), all names that have been used for the only sizeable town on the 'Long Isle', the nerve centre of the Hebrides, now universally known as Stornoway.

A very helpful chap who seemed to be in charge of the yacht pontoons came to check that I was safely moored and warn me of the approaching gale. 'If the fishermen are right about the weather, you'll be here for a week,' he grinned. 'It'll give you a chance to get to know Lewis.'

When I revealed I had sailed into Stornoway as a lad on fishing boats and later was a keeper at the Butt of Lewis lighthouse and was making a nostalgic return visit, he could not do enough for me. He promised to get me a bus timetable, help me to fill my water tanks if I needed it, and offered to drive me to the local supermarket; though I had to curb his enthusiasm when he talked of contacting the local newspaper.

12

LIFE IN A LIGHTHOUSE – THE BOCHAN – ACCUSED OF BEING A SPY

My experience of living on Lewis began with a visit to the offices of the Northern Lighthouse Board in Edinburgh in 1956, to be interviewed for my suitability as a trainee lighthouse keeper. To check I was not illiterate and to test my knowledge of geography, I was required to fill in the names of places like the Moray Firth and Orkney and Shetland on an outline map of Scotland, and the office manager seemed impressed when he read on my application form that, at the age of fifteen, I had sailed all round the Hebrides on trawlers and was familiar with many of the lighthouses.

'Do you know the Butt of Lewis?' he challenged.

'Yes,' I answered, 'a red-brick tower. One flash every five seconds.'

'Good,' he smiled. 'Now you'll get a closer look at it. That's where we're sending you.'

Two days later, by way of a train to Mallaig, MacBrayne's steamer the *Loch Seaforth* to Stornoway, and a rickety bus to Eoropie, a community at the top of the island, I arrived at the lighthouse. The following morning, eager to explore this strange land of stone houses with thatched roofs – many 'black houses' were still lived in – I borrowed the assistant keeper's bike and had hardly gone a mile when, from croft after croft, old ladies rushed out, screaming at me in Gaelic and hurling lumps of peat at my head.

Scared that I might have strayed near the local madhouse, I pedalled as fast as I could back to the lighthouse and learnt that, although I had been on Lewis barely twenty-four hours, I had offended the most powerful influence on the island, the

Free Presbyterian Church. And they were not going to let me off lightly either. At the next church meeting I was 'called' from the pulpit for riding a bicycle on the Lord's Day, a severe form of social disgrace in those days. I wondered if I had landed in a place where they still burnt witches at the stake.

Being publicly denounced for something as trivial as riding a bike on a Sunday, and finding that the islanders were not allowed to cook a meal on the Sabbath, that youngsters were banned from laughing, singing, listening to the radio or playing games, and that many people drew blinds over their windows and spent the day reading the Bible, I seemed to have come upon a bizarre way of life.

To try and understand this peculiar brand of religion, I read what I could about it and discovered that a breakaway group, who were disenchanted with the way the Church of Scotland was run, formed the Free Church of Scotland in the so-called Disruption of 1843. But they still could not find 'the peace of God that passeth all understanding'; and discontent rumbled on in the Free Church until, fifty years later, two ministers from Shieldaig on the mainland and a schoolmaster from the Island of Raasay, close to Skye, resolved 'to form themselves into a separate Presbytery not owning jurisdiction of the courts of the presently subsisting church calling herself the Free Church of Scotland'.

And so the Free Presbyterian Church, better known as the 'Wee Free', was founded and, with its puritanical brand of religion, held the islands of Lewis, Harris and North Uist in its unyielding grip. In 1896 William MacKay, an Inverness teacher, commenting on the power and influence of the Free Church, was worried that 'It has to a great extent destroyed the songs and tales which were the wonderfully pure intellectual pastimes of our fathers; it has suppressed innocent customs and recreations . . . and it has with its iron hand crushed merriment and good fellowship out of the souls of the people, and in their place planted an unhealthy gloominess and dread of the future entirely foreign to the nature of the Celt.'

Lewis had changed very little in a century when I was at the lighthouse in the 1950s but the world was developing rapidly and change was inevitable; and when I returned six decades later in *Halcyon*, I found that the 21st-century Gaels had finally rebelled and successfully campaigned to establish a Sunday ferry service from Stornoway to the mainland.

It was a decision that rocked Lewis and Harris, and even some of the rebels acknowledged that it would be unfortunate if the church that had done the most to preserve the Gaelic language were to lose the support of the islanders completely. But on my first night back in Stornoway, when I went for a walk round the town after my evening meal it was clear that the Free Presbyterian Church was by no means beaten. A large notice attached to a new public toilet block thundered, 'This toilet is closed on Sundays.'

The wind screeched through the rigging all night causing the mooring warps to creak and groan so much it was impossible to sleep, and around midnight I made a mug of coffee and switched on the VHF to check if any fishing boats were still at sea. Inevitably there were several, and in a string of obscenities I gathered that it was gusting to effing force ten in the effing Minch and the effing seas were as high as effing Ben Nevis, and there was no chance of catching any effing fish in this effing weather. The casual listener would be shocked by it, but having experienced terrifying wind and sea conditions on trawlers in the quest to keep fishmongers in business, I knew the strain on skippers was enormous, and venting their feelings with naughty words was their way of coping with nervous tension.

It was still blowing hard when the streaks of dawn began to light the sky, and I pulled my oilies on and ventured out to investigate the bangs and crashes I had heard during the night. *Halcyon*'s sails were well lashed down and had not moved, but the light cord lashings on the sails of two local yachts moored nearby had been blown to shreds and the sails with them. The row of fenders on a fine old varnished motor cruiser had snapped off, and I fished a couple of them out of the water and re-tied them to prevent the steel edge of the pontoon sawing its way into the hull. Apart from that, there was very little obvious damage and, unable to retrieve the numerous fenders and plastic fuel containers drifting around with the tide, I went back to the warmth of my sleeping bag.

I had a pan balanced on the stove frying eggs and bacon for my breakfast about 8.30 a.m. when I heard someone clamber aboard, and the cheery face of the pontoon master appeared at the hatch. 'Here's a bus timetable,' he said, handing me a printed sheet. 'You'll be able to get to the Butt today. The wind's moderated a bit. Did you have a wild night?'

I told him I had been listening to the fishing boats on the radio.

'Aye, it's no fun for them,' he replied. 'I heard there was a trawler in trouble in heavy seas about fifty miles west of Lewis and the rescue helicopter has gone out to try and lift the crew off. Poor sods.'

Borrowing my boathook, he went off to recover what fenders and fuel cans he could reach around the pontoons and to retie the warps of the moored yachts. I finished my breakfast and packed my rucksack with a flask, sandwiches and cameras, and walked down into the town to catch the bus to Eoropie and the Butt of Lewis. Due to one of those peculiar local anomalies where the departure time of a bus appears to have little connection with the timetable, I found I had just missed one bus and had an hour to wait for another. The warmth of several nearby cafes beckoned but, braving the wind, I wandered over to the fish dock to look at the brightly painted trawlers.

It was to the herring – the 'King of the Sea' – that Stornoway owed its reputation as a premier fishing port, and the old-timers used to say that in its heyday the herring shoals were so dense that boats were in danger of capsizing when their nets were being hauled in, and on the shore people were able to scoop the fish out of the water with their hands.

The fishing fleet grew to over a thousand boats, and herrings cured and barrelled in the port were shipped throughout Europe and Scandinavia. But right from the early days, the Scottish fishing grounds were being exploited by Spanish and Dutch fishermen and, as UK politicians were no wiser then than they are now, nothing was done to safeguard Scottish interests and as the fish stocks declined, so did the prosperity of centres like Stornoway.

The frantically busy harbour, crowded with boats and crews, that I had sailed into as a boy was now barely recognisable. There were no Russian fish buyers scooping a mug of brine out of a barrel and tasting it to check the quality of the herring; no irate skippers to be heard arguing with a grocer over the price of the stores delivered to his boat. Gone were the high-pitched voices of fish salesmen shouting for bids, the roar of engines being tested, and in the evenings the drunken dockside brawls, the screams and shouts and the sound of breaking glass.

After a weekend in Stornoway, getting the crew sober enough to put to sea again on Monday was always a problem for the fleet owners, and after scouring the pubs in search of his crew, my skipper used to say, 'Stornoway is an easy harbour to sail into, but it's a hell of a difficult one to sail out of.'

On the quay a fussy little forklift truck was busy loading an enormous refrigerated lorry that had travelled all the way from Spain.

'It's a crazy world, pal,' said a fisherman when I asked what the truck was doing in Stornoway. 'For years, the bloody Spaniards have been raiding our fishing grounds, but now if it wasn't for them the creel boats that work around the islands would have gone bust long ago. It doesn't make sense to me that they can drive thousands of miles from the south coast of Spain for a load of scrawny spider crabs from the Scottish islands, but they do, and the longer it lasts the better. It's helping to pay my mortgage.'

To kill time while waiting for the bus, I wandered around the side streets and came across the office of the Harris Tweed Association and, as it was conveniently sheltered from the wind, I studied the promotional photographs in the windows and read the optimistic forecasts for the future of tweed. In an age geared up to the latest computer technology, it seemed amazing that, tucked away in little sheds all over Lewis and Harris and other Hebridean islands, there were men to be found laboriously weaving tweed on antiquated handlooms. The name 'Harris' tweed often causes confusion since Lewis is the main weaving and processing centre, and it is also woven on several other Hebridean islands, but its fame was all due to Catherine, Countess of Dunmore, the same lady who had the willy on the male statue at Rodel removed by gunfire.

Her husband inherited Harris from his father in 1836 and, deeply moved by the distress of the people caused by poverty, she organised sales in London of the tweed made in Harris, and the name evolved naturally. It was due to her energy and enthusiasm that the Harris tweed industry was founded, and a legal case in the 1960s upheld the definition of Harris tweed, which excluded mainland producers: 'A tweed made from pure virgin wool, produced in Scotland, spun, dyed and finished in the Outer Hebrides, and hand-woven by the Islanders at their own homes in the Islands of Lewis, Harris, Uist, Barra, and their several purtenancies, and all known as the Outer Hebrides.'

The trademark of the Harris Tweed Association, the orb and Maltese cross, was taken from the Countess of Dunmore's coat of arms, and cannot be used by anyone else. The promotional material was very upbeat, but reading between the lines I got the impression of an industry that was clinging to the edge of a precipice by its fingernails and was desperately in need of a lifeline in the form of substantial orders.

Leaving the Harris Tweed Association to its struggle to survive in a world that would rather have cheap man-made fibre than quality hand-woven woollen cloth, I braved the gale and found a shop that sold batteries that would enable me to continue to use my cameras until I could buy a new battery charger. There was still no sign of the bus when I struggled back to the bus stop, and no shelter either; but just when I was certain that every drop of blood in my body had been frozen solid by the wind and I would have to make a life-saving dash to a cafe for a hot drink, there was a toot on a horn and the bus emerged from a side street and wheezed to a halt.

Still with a picture in my mind of the 1950s and the bus packed with women returning home with baskets overflowing with groceries, I was surprised how few local people were waiting for it. The queue consisted mostly of backpackers, Stornoway-based hotel guests on a day excursion, and an elderly American couple who let it be known, in that uninhibited way Americans have, that they were hot on the trail of a croft in Port of Ness where their ancestors had lived.

Beyond Stornoway, the hinterland of Lewis is a landscape you either love or hate. There is no compromise. For mile after mile after mile there is a vast expanse of bleak, featureless, treeless, invariably wet and windy, undulating peat bog, relieved at intervals close to the road by the houses and narrow green fields of the crofting communities.

Never was this more apparent than when seen through the window of the bus as it trundled along the road leading north from Stornoway, crossing twelve miles of moorland almost to the coast at Barvas on the west side, before making a right-angled turn and keeping parallel with the coast for another fourteen miles until it reached the widespread northernmost communities of Port of Ness, Lionel and Eoropie, the dropping-off point for the mile-long track to the towering headland of Rubha Robhanais (Butt of Lewis).

The gale-force wind almost bowled me over when I stepped down from the bus at Eoropie and, bent double and gasping for breath, I fought my way along the track to the lighthouse. Drawing near to the familiar red-brick tower, I could hear the awesome boom of the giant waves as they slammed into the cliffs, and could taste the salt spray that was being blasted high into the air. Reaching the squat buildings of the keepers' houses, I could barely conceal my excitement. I knew that the lighthouse had been automated and was no longer manned, and I had conditioned myself for change, but I was horrified when I saw the extent of the abandonment.

The whitewashed walls and painted doors and windows were neglected, cracked and peeling, and the vegetable gardens and lawns, tended meticulously by generations of keepers, were overgrown with a wild tangle of weeds. A man came out of a building and eyed me suspiciously, but when I explained that I had been a keeper at the lighthouse in the 1950s he greeted me warmly and, though visitors were no longer allowed to go up the tower, he unlocked the door for me. 'You're different,' he said with a laugh, 'and I'm sure you'll know the way.'

Reaching behind the door, he pressed a switch and the inside of the tower was instantly lit with electric light. 'I bet you didn't have anything like that in your day,' he said. How right he was – paraffin lamps ruled in the 1950s – but at least we never had a power cut! I climbed slowly up the spiral of over one hundred stone steps and a short, steep ladder to the room that housed the light mechanism; but the simple large, pressurised paraffin lamp with a mantle that I was familiar with had gone, and in its place was a giant electric bulb.

Gone too was the clockwork mechanism that had revolved the huge glass prism of the lantern around the mantle without a hitch, and with the minimum of effort and maintenance had sent a searing flash of light twenty-five miles out into the black wilderness of the Atlantic Ocean every five seconds between dusk and dawn for over a hundred years.

Yet technical whiz-kids had talked the Northern Lighthouse Board and their political masters into believing that, by replacing the mantle with an electric lamp and the clockwork mechanism with an electric motor, and controlling both from an office hundreds of miles away, the job could be done more efficiently.

Bella Bathurst, in her superbly researched book, *The Lighthouse Stevensons*, about the legendary dynasty of lighthouse builders, quotes Captain James Taylor of the Northern Lighthouse Board as saying that the Stevensons would have approved of automation; but with his political bosses breathing down his neck it was not likely he would have said anything else.

The Stevensons were fastidious engineers and lighthouse builders dedicated to excellence and, instead of grieving over a trail of neglected and crumbling eyesores left behind in the wake of automation, they might just as well have preferred to maintain the status quo, in the knowledge that the lights and the buildings around them were in the caring hands of an extremely dedicated band of men, for whom being a lighthouse keeper was more than a job; it was a way of life!

With a last glance out of the lantern-room window, from where I had watched the Atlantic Ocean at its ugliest and most horrifying when winter hurricanes churned the sea into a boiling cauldron of foam and caused the massive 37 metre lighthouse tower to sway slightly, I went back down to the yard and startled my caretaker friend by asking him if the Bochan was still being used. With a wrinkled frown he said, 'Och, yes, it is still there and still the den of Satan it always was. I hope you will not be going there. Many a good man the Bochan has ruined.'

In Gaelic the word *bothan*, pronounced bochan, is a shebeen or illegal drinking den; and, thanks to the refusal of the Free Church to allow a properly licensed and regulated village pub, it served as a gathering place for the men and had an unsavoury reputation for marathon drinking sessions. Anyone who frequented it was considered a social outcast by the good and proper, but the men went anyway. There was nowhere else to have an all-male social gathering.

Burning to visit this mysterious meeting-house which men were reluctant to mention in front of their wives, I had asked Calum, an assistant keeper at the lighthouse and a man who knew the Bochan well, if he would take me; and on a dark, starry night with the aroma of peat smoke hanging in the air, I followed the dim, red rear light of his bike along the winding roads until we turned off down a rocky lane and stopped in front of a small, windowless 'black house'.

When I stepped through the low door the men inside froze, but Calum quickly explained who I was in Gaelic. The inside of the building had been 'modified' with a pot-bellied stove in the centre of the earth floor and wooden benches built around the walls. The air was thick with cigarette and pipe smoke that swirled round a pressurised paraffin lamp suspended from a roof beam, and the heat from the peat-filled stove was stifling.

The benches were well filled but Calum managed to find two vacant places, and a man I recognised as a local fisherman handed me a generous glass of whisky. Several crates of a well-known brand of whisky were stacked in a corner, and Calum said it was bought in Stornoway and the men paid for it by the glass at a fraction of the price it would have cost in the town.

'But don't be drinking that!' he whispered, pointing to several bottles and jars of different sizes full of a clear liquid that looked like water. 'That's the stuff they make in a still on the moor, and it'll blow your head off.'

'If it's that powerful, who drinks it?' I whispered back.

'Och, well, some of the hard cases can drink it but it's usually mixed with a bought whisky, and even then it can give you a headache you'll remember for a long time.'

A giant of a man got to his feet and, with his glass held high and drumming a foot slowly on the floor, started to sing a Gaelic song. Calum said it was a song about going to sea in a small boat and, when the rest of the room joined in and the voices rose and fell, the atmosphere was so charged I imagined I could feel the movement of the boat butting into the seas. Several songs followed, in which the men either sang with the giant or joined in the chorus, and then there was a lull while glasses were recharged.

'I hope you've got a good stomach,' Calum grinned. 'We're about to have the gugas.'

'The what?' I said in surprise.

'The gugas,' Calum repeated. 'They're young gannets. The Port of Ness men go out every year to Sula Sgeir, an island about forty miles north of the Butt, and they gather up the young gannets and pickle 'em in salt. To eat them they have to be boiled, and one of the lads has brought a few with him.'

A space was cleared on the benches, and a fierce-looking character with a large knife began sawing several headless boiled seabirds into chunks and passing them round the room. My portion had been relayed by numerous grubby hands before it reached me, but with twenty pairs of eyes watching my reaction I accepted it cheerfully, though it took all my courage to bite into the foul-smelling, greasy lump of flesh that had once been a gannet. It was meat that had the smell and taste of fish, and my stomach threatened to react; but, helped down with gulps of whisky, I finally managed to swallow every piece.

Calum and the rest of the men tucked into theirs as if it were prime steak, and sat swaying happily with a whisky in one hand and a chunk of guga in the other, while grease dribbled down their chins. The men were singing a Gaelic love song when we left to bike back to the lighthouse and, though I had difficulty in steering a straight line, I would not have missed my one and only visit to a bochan for anything; it was a side of island life few outsiders have ever experienced.

When the local doctor heard of my escapade, he thought I had been drinking the home-made stuff and sent me a warning letter, enclosing a copy of Martin Martin's account of his visit to the islands in the 17th century in which he reported, 'The natives brew several sorts of liquors, a common usquebaugh, another called trestarig, three times distilled which is strong and hot: a third sort is four times distilled . . . which at first taste affects all members of the body; two spoonfuls of this last liquor is of sufficient dose; and if any man exceed this, it would presently stop his breath and endanger his life.'

I avoided mentioning to the lighthouse caretaker that I had once been in the Bochan, and he seemed highly relieved when I said I only wanted to photograph it. With the help of his directions I found it without difficulty, though I was surprised to see a small estate of new bungalows had been built close to it. It was exactly as

I remembered it, a typical small 'black house' with a thatched roof weighted down by large stones suspended in fishing nets on lengths of rope. As it was windowless I could not peep inside, but the newly painted door and the chimney pipe from the pot-bellied stove still poking defiantly through the thatch signalled that business at the Bochan was still very much alive.

With an hour to spare before I was due to catch the bus back to Stornoway, I walked down to Port of Ness to look at the harbour. Apart from Brevig, a purpose-built harbour for fishing boats in Broad Bay a few miles north of Stornoway, it was the only usable haven along the one hundred nautical miles of coast from Stornoway on the east side to East Loch Roag on the west side, yet it hardly rated a mention in Yachtsman's Pilots and there were no harbour plans. The Admiralty Pilot to the West of Scotland provided useful but brief information, probably because the big disadvantage of the harbour was that it dried out, but any yachtsman brave enough to venture along the harsh and unforgiving coast of Lewis might be very relieved to lie against its sheltered harbour wall if conditions were too tough to go round the Butt.

After a northerly gale it was a natural trap for interesting flotsam carried in on the huge swell and one day, while I was poking around among the usual baulks of timber and fish boxes during an off-duty watch at the lighthouse, I found a waterproof tube about a metre long by about fifteen centimetres in diameter. When I cut the seal and opened it, I was amazed to find a thick roll of slightly damp Russian sea charts of the Hebrides and the north of Scotland, and several pages of notes handwritten in Russian.

It was at the height of the Cold War with Russia, when we were brainwashed into believing that anything Russian was a threat to our security; and when I handed the charts to Sandy, the Principal Keeper, he went into a panic and immediately phoned the local policeman.

With the burst of urgency expected of a Hebridean police officer in times of national emergency, he arrived two days later on his bike and, having laboriously entered the details in his notebook of the time and place where the 'mysterious foreign property' had been discovered, he tied the tube of charts to his crossbar with a piece of string and nonchalantly pedalled away. I thought that was the end of the matter but, a week or so later, a large black car drew up at the lighthouse and I was summoned to the Principal Keeper's house.

'These gentlemen have come all the way from London and want to ask you a few questions,' said Sandy nervously.

The 'gentlemen' were a sour-faced, unsmiling duo, dressed identically in belted grey raincoats and trilby hats, and looked so like characters from an Ian Fleming novel I half expected them to introduce themselves as 007 and 008. Seated behind the Principal's desk and ordering me to stand, 007, obviously the senior of the two, began to interrogate me as if I were a spy.

What was my name?

Where was I born?

Were my parents British?

Had I ever been to Russia?

Had I any friends in Russia?

008 had a transcript of the local policeman's notes and he flung it on the desk like a trump card. 'When you opened the container and looked at the charts, how did you know the language was Russian?' he demanded.

'Well, that's easy,' I replied. 'I once had a girlfriend who was studying Russian at university. She wanted to be an interpreter.' It was the wrong thing to have said. They both sat bolt upright.

'You knew someone who was studying Russian?' hissed 007, as if I had just confessed to a horrible crime.

008 leapt to his feet. 'And you allowed this person to read the papers in the tube?' he challenged.

'Hardly,' I said, 'the last I heard of her she had married an Australian and was living in Sydney.'

For an hour they grilled me with questions as if trying to get me to confess I was a Russian 'plant', and even drove me down to the harbour to point out the exact spot where I had found the tube. They made it very clear they thought I was not telling them everything and when, in answer to the question, 'Have you seen any submarines on the surface?' I replied, 'Yes, occasionally,' it only increased their suspicions. Finally 008 took another tack, hinting that perhaps one of the submarines could have been from a 'hostile nation' and in future I should keep a sharp lookout in case it was liaising with one of the locals, and the charts were intended for him.

Sandy said it was ludicrous to think that any local could be a spy, but the pair only glared at him. Still sour-faced and unsmiling, and without a word of thanks to Sandy's wife for the tea and cake she had laid on for them, they announced they had finished their investigations and made ready to leave. As they walked to their car, a sudden gust of wind lifted 007's trilby hat high into the air, and he watched helplessly as it swirled out to sea and landed in the middle of the bay. With a touch of unconcealed mirth in his voice Sandy broke the silence. 'Och, well now gentlemen, what a terrible shame about the hat. But if it drifts over to Russia, do you think the Russians will waste as much time trying to find out where it came from as you have done with the charts?'

Without a word, 007 climbed into the car and, with 008 furiously scribbling notes on a pad, they drove back to Stornoway and the ferry to the mainland. We never heard any more about the charts.

Brightly painted modern bungalows and houses had done a lot to brighten up the once drab panorama of grey croft houses around Port of Ness, but it was with a tinge of sadness that I passed the ruins of a 'black house' I had once been invited into for tea. A part-time keeper at the lighthouse, Donald MacLeod, had taken me to meet the old couple who lived in it, and walking through their door was like stepping back in time.

The smoke from a peat fire smouldering in the middle of the earth floor made my eyes water, and for a few minutes I could hardly see. The old couple treated me like a long-lost son, and I was seated at a rough wooden table and plied with home-made oatcakes and butter, and cups of tea made with water boiled in a kettle hung on a chain over the peat fire.

The man was wearing the blue dungaree trousers and jacket popular with the island men at the time, but his wife wore a long-sleeved black dress, buttoned right up to her neck, which in the strictly regulated etiquette of island life in the 1950s seemed to be compulsory for any woman over fifty. It was a legacy from the 19th century, when a Lewis minister condemned the wearing of bright clothing, saying that it showed frivolous minds that endangered immortal souls. They had very little English, and while Donald chatted to them in Gaelic it gave me an opportunity to take in my surroundings.

With only two tiny windows in the massive, thick walls it was very dark inside the house, and the only outlet for the smoke from the fire was a hole in the thatched roof. Outside it was bitterly cold and blowing hard, yet I could scarcely hear the wind and, although the interior was extremely basic with very little furniture apart from the table and chairs, two fireside chairs, a sideboard and a dresser for storing crockery, it was remarkably warm and cosy. The living room also doubled up as a bedroom with a box bed, complete with curtains, built into a corner. Hanging on the rough walls were a few faded paintings of Lewis, sepia-toned family photographs, and a wood-framed, elaborately woven sampler with the legend 'God is Love' in English.

They had none of the amenities of modern houses. Water was carried in a bucket from a nearby well, the toilet was a dry privy in the Tigh-Beag (little house) outside, and an oil lamp and candles were the only form of lighting. I imagined it on a winter's night when the neighbours came in for a ceilidh (a visit) and crowded round the fire to talk and sing and tell the stories that had been passed down through generations. When it was time for us to leave, the couple clasped my hands warmly and the wife said something in Gaelic. Donald told me afterwards it was a Gaelic blessing.

Sixty years on, squinting through the viewfinder of my camera, I imagined the old couple waving from their doorway, but when I looked again all I could see was a desolate ruin with collapsed walls and rotting roof timbers, silhouetted against

Top left: The author, Bob Orrell

Top right: Pip Siddle, almost a tall as the mizzen mast

Above: Loch Ranza Castle, Arran

Above: Staffa and Fingal's Cave
Below: Castlebay, Barra

Above: A blackhouse on North Uist

Below: Eriskay, South Uist in the background

Above: Wizard pool, North Uist

Below: Rodel harbour

Opposite page: Callanish Stones, Lewis

Jaw bone of a whale, Bragar, Lewis

Above: An unforgiving coast, West Lewis

Right: Calum MacKay weaving Harris tweed, Port of Ness, Lewis

Above: Butt of Lewis lighthouse
Below: 'Can't let that fish go to waste' – a seal in Stornoway harbour
Opposite page: Port of Ness harbour

Above: The fish quay, Gairloch
Below: A mountain backdrop, Loch Torridon
Opposite page: Stornoway harbour

Above: Shieldaig village, Loch Torridon
Below: Sunset, Loch Torridon
Opposite page: Acarseid Mhor anchorage, Rona

Above: Arisaig harbour, Isle of Eigg on the right
Below: Tobermory, Mull

Above: Passing the sail training ship 'Lord Nelson' near Oban
Below: A westerly gale in Loch Craignish

Rothesay harbour, Isle of Bute

the sky. It had been a rare glimpse of another part of Hebridean life that has gone for ever, and remembered only in tourist brochures and folk museums.

Curious to see if the local shop had survived the supermarket onslaught, I walked along to the little community of Lionel, half expecting to see another blackened ruin; but, though it was still in business, the old shop had new owners and was not the same without 'Big Donald' presiding over it.

In his youth Donald had sailed to Canada, and had been almost buried under a mountain of grain while unloading a ship in the Yukon with Robert Service, who became famous as the Yukon poet. Had it not been for Donald's exceptional reach that enabled him to grab a rope, the world would have lost a fine poet and Lewis a genial raconteur. I had earned his undying gratitude when the petrol engine powering his ancient sausage machine sheared a toothed drive wheel. The machine was as old as Methuselah and it was impossible to get spares for it. When I painstakingly made a new drive wheel from blanks kept in the lighthouse workshop for such emergencies, he was so overjoyed he presented me with a huge home-made haggis the size of a football.

Watching Donald, clad in blood-stained Wellington boots and a sacking apron, making haggis in his back shed would have had today's Environmental Health Inspectors howling with disbelief, but for taste and flavour there was no equal. Though a master of his trade in the butchery department, Donald was less knowledgeable on the grocery side, and got himself into a fluster one day when the wife of a local dignitary, who had just moved to Lewis from the mainland came into the shop. She was from a smart suburb of Edinburgh and liked to let it be known that she was a cut above the islanders, and only mixed with people of the right social standing. 'Donald!' she declared in her best 'plum in the mouth' accent, 'I'm having a dinner party tonight for some influential friends, and they've absolutely demanded that I make one of my mouth-watering meals. Have you any Cremola?'

'Och, well now, Cremola,' said Donald slowly, scratching his head. 'Cremola,' he repeated. He had clearly never heard of it, but wanting to please, he said briskly, 'Wait you a minute now,' and disappeared into his back store. There was the sound of boxes crashing to the floor and muffled curses in Gaelic, then he emerged, dishevelled and covered in cobwebs, but with a triumphant smile on his face. 'Well now, I'm sorry Mrs McKenzie, I haven't the Cremola,' he said, 'but I have Harpic,' and he handed her a bottle of the popular lavatory cleaner.

I bought a copy of the local newspaper in the shop, and was sitting against a wall sheltered from the wind browsing through it when the Stornoway bus appeared and I flagged it down and clambered on board. The elderly American couple who had been tracing their ancestors were sitting on the back seat holding hands like two lovers.

'Did you find your family house?' I asked.

'Sure did,' replied the man, turning to his wife and planting a big kiss on her cheek.

'It's in poor shape but we're fixing to buy it and maybe come home, ain't we honey?'

His wife smiled in agreement and, spreading a plan of the old croft house across their laps, they chattered about it like two excited children.

When the bus pulled away I sank back into a seat and stared gloomily out of the window, pondering on whether it had been a wise move to go back to a place so full of poignant memories of happy times; but I was saved from lapsing into melancholia when the bus drove past the house where the local policeman had lived with his wife. It stirred the memory of the time when I took him a few trout by way of thanks for lending me books about Lewis. I often fished for trout in one of the lochs on the moor, which was quite lawful, but occasionally I bagged a few grouse with a shotgun, which was not. I used the same game bag for both activities and when I arrived at the policeman's door with the trout, his wife called, 'Come on in and put them on the kitchen table.'

Without thinking, I upended the bag on the table, and out fell the fish along with a flurry of grouse feathers. I stared at them horrified, hardly daring to move, and there was a long silence while the policeman gazed at the feathers settling gently towards his floor. Then he looked at me and with a voice dripping with sarcasm – though I could see his face was twitching with laughter – said, 'Och, I see it's the flying fish you've been catching. I've fished that loch many times myself and never knew they were there. Wait you till I tell the estate factor, he'll have the visitors paying big money to try their luck!' He winked at his wife and went on, 'I'll have to report this to the Superintendent, and maybe the *Stornoway Gazette* would like to hear about the Lewis flying fish that have feathers like a grouse.' Picking up one of the fish he turned to me. 'Will we need to pluck them or will they grill like ordinary trout?'

Squirming with embarrassment, I ran for the door and I could still hear him rocking with laughter when I was a long way down the road.

Browsing through the bus timetable while we bumped and lurched our way along the coast road, I discovered that if I got off at Barvas before the bus turned inland for Stornoway I could catch another bus that continued along the coast following a twenty-five-mile scenic route back to the town.

When I mentioned it to the driver he called it 'the tourist trail', and with a roguish grin said I should look out for the whalebone arch at Bragar, the Broch at Carloway, and the famous Callanish standing stones, then I could boast I had 'done' Lewis. He stopped at the junction of the road to Stornoway and the 'scenic route' to pick up a party of hikers, and with a wave to the American couple I stepped down onto the road. I had only walked a few metres when the next bus appeared bang on time, bulging with visitors of so many different nationalities it was like a mobile United Nations.

At Bragar, the famed whalebone arch formed a conspicuous and unusual entrance to the driveway of a large house and had a grotesque harpoon hanging from it. It would not have impressed any fan of Greenpeace, but it appealed to the Japanese and Norwegians on the bus and they photographed it frantically through the windows until it had disappeared from view. I often saw large schools of whales close to the Butt of Lewis, including the feared 'killer' whale, and the locals of Port of Ness said that in days gone by they were much sought after as a source of food.

'They call it sea pork', wrote Martin Martin in the 17th century. 'The natives employed many boats together in pursuit of the whales, chasing them into the bays … there were fifty young whales killed in this manner, and most of them eaten by the common people, who by experience find them to be a very nourishing food.'

But whale hunting had its hazards. Martin reported that a large whale overturned one of the boats and devoured three of the crew. Usually only associated with the colder latitudes, whaling continued off the west coast of Lewis right up to fairly recent times, and the arch was the jawbone of a blue whale that had been washed ashore at Bragar in 1920. The harpoon that killed it was still attached to its body. The unfortunate whale must have endured an agonising death but, thankfully, more and more countries are becoming aware of the need to protect these graceful giants of the sea and, while in UK waters at least, they are safe from predators.

At Carloway the sight of the massive Broch dominating the skyline caused another international flurry of excitement and, shepherded by a perspiring and harassed lady guide who explained that their tour minibus had broken down and she was having to use public transport, the multilingual assortment of camera-clickers poured off the bus and I had it to myself.

Looking for all the world like a stone-built conical beehive, the Broch was the nuclear fallout shelter of its time where, in the event of an attack by hostile clans intent on murder and mayhem, the whole community could take refuge inside and wall up the entrance. It was a popular attraction on the 'tourist trail' but, depending on the arrival of their repaired minibus, the international party's ultimate 'must see' was another five miles down the road at the head of East Loch Roag.

Featured on hundreds of calendars and picture postcards, the mystical standing stones of Callanish rival Stonehenge as the most important prehistoric site in the UK, and have for long kept academics and archaeologists arguing about who put the stones there and why. Called Teampull na Greine (Temple of the Sun) by the Gaels and 'The Great Winged Temple of the Northern Isles' by Greek scholars, it is said to date back to 1500 BC. I first wandered around the site when I was a keeper at the Butt of Lewis and counted over forty upright slabs of gnarled rock, varying from two metres high to a solitary giant of five metres, which were set out in a huge area in the shape of a Celtic cross.

Some ghoulish types like to believe that on Midsummer's Day the sun-worshipping Druids, clad in their white robes, gathered in a circle and, when the sun reached a certain angle, the Chief Druid plunged his dagger into the heart of a human sacrifice lying on an altar. Others say that is baloney; there is no evidence that Druids did anything of the sort and the stones probably had more to do with celebrating fertility and the seasons. And so the controversy rages on, but it brings the tourists in, and the knick-knack shops and tearooms do very nicely out of it.

From Callanish, the predominant feature of the twelve miles of switchback road that joins the west coast of Lewis to the east coast is a rolling expanse of peat bog peppered with a myriad tiny lochs, and though it would hardly have won an award for the world's most outstanding landscape it had a raw beauty, and at one point was given a 'Landseer' effect by a magnificent red deer stag who held up the bus by haughtily posing in the middle of the road with his harem of hinds. To get a good view of the scenery I moved to a front seat near the driver, and on the outskirts of Stornoway we witnessed at first hand the power of fervent prayer.

Climbing a hill, the bus was obliged to fall in behind a coach full of schoolchildren who were having a jolly time making lewd gestures to passing motorists. But they made the mistake of directing one of their depraved signs towards a driver who, from his clerical collar, was obviously a man of the church and who must have called for divine retribution. The coach suddenly braked hard and pulled into the side and, as we drove past, a line of ashen-faced youngsters were being violently sick onto the grass.

13

FLANNAN ISLES TRAGEDY – MCDRUG – CROSSING THE MINCH

The wind was still gusting around the yacht pontoons and it had started to rain when I got back to *Halcyon*. After half an hour of struggling to light the cabin stove I huddled close to it and helped the warmth to spread with a mug of coffee and a large dram. A day wallowing in nostalgia had drained me. I longed to escape from people and with *Halcyon* under full sail get on with what the poet Wordsworth described as 'breaking the silence of the seas, among the farthest Hebrides'.

I even pulled out the charts with the intention of leaving there and then, but a sudden VHF radio alarm from Stornoway Coastguard scuppered the reckless move with a warning of another imminent gale. When I tuned in to the BBC, the forecaster on Radio Scotland was very apologetic about it, but said the area of intense low pressure would cross the country quickly and be followed by a ridge of high pressure and a few days of settled weather. Too weary to cook a meal, I settled for a couple of cheese sandwiches, crawled into my sleeping bag and slept a dreamless sleep until I was shaken awake by a tremendous crash on deck.

Glancing at my watch, it was 3 a.m.; a full gale was howling through the rigging and torrential rain battered the skylight. Pulling oilies over my pyjamas I grabbed a torch, went on deck, and saw that a fibreglass dinghy had been blown off a nearby boat and was neatly impaled on *Halcyon*'s samson post on the foredeck. There was nothing I could do about it, so I went back to my sleeping bag until the owner of the dinghy roused me at 10 a.m., ruefully asking if he and a friend could retrieve it.

The gale and rain raged all morning, and to get away from the noise I went ashore to the local library and was absorbed in the blood-letting, clan warfare, periods of prosperity and missed opportunities that were the history of the island of Lewis, when the elderly American couple I had met the previous day on the bus came in to browse through old newspapers.

They told me they were researching the Flannan Isles tragedy, and I was fascinated to discover that the woman was related to one of the lighthouse keepers who, with two other keepers, had mysteriously disappeared off the remote Flannan Isles, eighteen miles west of Lewis, in December 1900. They knew very little about it other than that the man's name was Donald McArthur, and I suggested they contact the archives of the Northern Lighthouse Board in Edinburgh, who might have more information about their relative.

The story of the Flannan Isles mystery when three lighthouse keepers disappeared without trace has been told in many, often wildly fanciful, versions, and even had a poem written about it. But the captain of the Northern Lighthouse Board's ship that first discovered the tragedy happened to be the uncle of Sandy, the Principal Keeper when I was at the Butt of Lewis, so I was able to get a 'no frills' account of events.

At midnight on 15 December 1900, the steamer *Archtor* passed close to the Flannan Isles and the captain noted in his log that the light was not working, but coasting ships did not carry radio equipment in those days and he was not able to report it until reaching port some time later. Meantime, the Northern Lighthouse Board's ship *Hesperus* had left Oban bound for the Board's base at Breasclete, near Callanish in East Loch Roag, on the west side of Lewis, to pick up relief keeper Joseph Moore, then carry on to the Flannans to land Moore and stores.

The ship was delayed by bad weather, and did not arrive until Boxing Day off Eilean Mor, the island of the Flannans group on which the lighthouse had been built only a year earlier; but, despite repeated blasts of the ship's whistle and the firing of a rocket, there was no sign of life and a boat was lowered to investigate. It managed to land Joseph Moore at some steps on the sheltered east side of the island, and he went up to the lighthouse and checked all the rooms and shouted for the keepers; but there was only an eerie silence.

Terrified, he ran back to the landing and, when the second mate and two crewmen returned with him, they entered the lamp room and found that the lamp had been cleaned and was ready for lighting. Reading through the log book, Moore found that it had been completed up to 13 December, and other notes intended to be written in later were recorded on a slate at 9 a.m. on 15 December, the day the light was reported as not working.

Even more puzzling was that the oilskins and sea boots belonging to James Ducat, the principal keeper, and Thomas Marshall, an assistant keeper, were missing; yet the jacket of Donald McArthur, the occasional keeper, was still hanging on a peg, indicating that he had probably gone out in his shirtsleeves. The crew scoured the island, but not a trace of the three men could be found, and the only clues to what might have happened were at the boat landing on the west side.

A box, bolted to the rock thirty-four metres above the sea, and used to store rope and tackle, had been swept away, and the ropes strewn in crevices in the rocks. Iron railings were twisted or had been torn from their foundations, a lifebuoy had been ripped from its stand and destroyed, and a block of stone, estimated to weigh over a ton, had been dislodged and hurled down onto the landing steps.

Leaving Moore and two crewmen to man the light until relief keepers were available, the *Hesperus* returned to East Loch Roag, from where the captain telegraphed the grim findings to the Board's office in Edinburgh:

'A dreadful accident has happened at the Flannans. The three keepers, Ducat, Marshall and the Occasional, have disappeared from the island.'

The Flannan Isles had always been regarded as a holy and mystical place, and in ancient times the people of Uig on Lewis made an annual pilgrimage to worship in St Flannan's chapel on Eilean Mor. The superstitious islanders let their imaginations run riot with stories about the keepers having been spirited away; but after a detailed examination of the boat landing, the Board's Superintendent, Robert Muirhead, took a less hysterical view and concluded that the men had been washed off the landing by a freak wave on the afternoon of 15 December, the day the captain of the steamer *Archtor* had noticed that the light was not working.

The lighthouse on the Flannan Isles is now fully automatic and the island is uninhabited. Only St Flannan and his ghostly disciples know what took place on that fateful day in December 1900. The official theory that they were swept away by a wave seemed to be confirmed when a descendant of one of the families who were evacuated from St Kilda in the 1930s said that his grandfather used to talk about the day when he and some men were out fishing in a boat off the island of Hirta, just after Christmas in 1900, and saw three bodies floating on the sea, two of them wearing uniforms with brass buttons. Being highly superstitious, they considered it bad luck to go near them and they rowed away.

By mid-afternoon there was every sign that the stormy, low-pressure system was moving away when the rain eased to a drizzle and the gale-force wind faded to barely a whisper; and keen for a leg stretch I left the library and walked across a bridge near the yacht pontoons into the wooded grounds of Lews Castle, once the home of James Matheson, the MP for Ross and Cromarty who bought Lewis and Harris from the ill-fated Seaforths. For centuries the Hebrides had been a Viking stronghold, but the Norse warriors rather tainted their contribution to the annals of Lewis by torching the ancient forests and leaving the island treeless. It was not until Matheson arrived in 1844, built his imposing house at the edge of the town and imported thousands of tons of soil, that anyone had taken a serious interest in re-planting trees.

Wandering along the delightful paths among the trees and flowerbeds, it was easy to imagine Matheson and his lady strolling along and enjoying their island hideaway, but there were many who resented his position, not least Prime Minister Disraeli, who spitefully dubbed him 'McDrug' because he had made his fortune from the opium trade in China. He was not afraid of spending it, though, and lavished huge sums of money on improving Stornoway town and the quay, bringing relief to the people of Lewis when the potato crop failed and there was severe famine, between 1845 and 1850.

But like so many landowners in the Hebrides, the Mathesons were never able to connect with the people and, weary of years of agitation from locals for land to be given up for crofting, the Matheson family sold Lewis in 1917 to Lord Leverhulme, the soap tycoon, followed by Harris in 1919.

Nicknamed Bodach an t-Siabuin (the Soap Man) by the islanders, Leverhulme was a marketing genius, but his well-intentioned, though misguided, attempts to win the hearts of the natives by pouring hundreds of thousands of pounds into developing a major fishing industry on Lewis failed. Disillusioned, the noble lord took his money and boundless enthusiasm down to Harris, where he invested in the whale-processing plant in West Loch Tarbert, but the men of Harris were no more enthusiastic about his ideas than the men of Lewis. To this day controversy smoulders about whether the islanders should have supported Leverhulme's attempts to strengthen the economy of Lewis and Harris.

Leverhulme's parting gesture to Stornoway in 1923 was the gift of Lews Castle, and I was taking photographs of it when an elderly man walking a dog tottered by and said jokingly, 'Be quick with your photographs – it might fall down any time, it's in a bad state of repair.' While doing his best to prevent his dog from cocking its leg against my camera tripod, he told me that the castle had once been used as a college where he had studied navigation before going to sea, and when he retired he was the captain of a large passenger liner. 'The old castle's become a bit of a liability since then,' he said, 'and if some members of the Trust had their way they'd get the bulldozers in, but they can't do it because of the terms of Leverhulme's gift to the town.'

He was keen to tell me more, but his dog had finally achieved its aim and peed over the legs of the tripod, and with a quick apology he dragged it away and hurried off towards the woods. 'The weather will be fine tomorrow,' he called, 'and you'll find sea conditions in the Minch a lot more settled than they have been.' I wondered why he had mentioned the sea conditions, then realised my oilskin suit, Breton cap and sea boots were a giveaway and he had guessed I was off a boat.

I tuned in to the weather forecast on BBC Radio Scotland that evening, and the old sea captain was right. The weather lady almost cooed with delight at the prospect of several days of warm weather ahead, and after a grand meal of genuine

Stornoway black pudding, joined in the pan by two eggs, a rasher of bacon and sauté potatoes, helped along with a glass of red wine, I spread the charts on the cabin table to work out a route that would take me across the Minch and south down the mainland coast, exploring the many sea lochs along the way.

I worked out a course to Loch Ewe, a touch over thirty nautical miles from Stornoway, with its wide entrance easily identified between the towering headlands of Greenstone Point and Rubha Réidh. First, though, I had to cross the Minch, which could be as fickle as a Scottish summer and rough when there was no reason for it to be rough. The BBC had pledged light winds, but Stornoway Coastguard's forecast for the Minch was more seamanlike, with a south-westerly wind force two to three, fair weather, good visibility and sea state slight to moderate.

The following day dawned bright and sunny and, with everything stowed away and the warps ready for casting off, I pressed the engine starter button. The starter motor gave a tired groan and then there was silence. I pressed again but nothing happened. The battery was dead flat and when I tested it with a voltmeter it showed zero. Fortunately the accessories battery that powered the cabin lights and the radios showed 'fully charged', and it was a matter of minutes to swap the batteries round.

This time the engine roared into life, but it was mystifying. One of the most useful bits of equipment, fitted to *Halcyon*'s mizzen mast, was a Marlec wind generator, and when under sail it had faithfully kept the batteries charged up and was utterly reliable. I tried charging the flat battery with a portable generator I carried for emergencies, but it was a waste of time, it was dead. I spent the morning scouring Stornoway, but I could not get the type of replacement I wanted unless I was prepared to wait for one to be delivered from the mainland, though I did find a shop that sold camera battery chargers and bought one. Clutching it like a trophy I returned to *Halcyon* and plugged it into the portable generator.

Reluctant to waste the good weather waiting for a new starter battery, I pulled away from the pontoons and followed a coastal tanker out of the harbour. Six hours later, after an uneventful crossing in a slight swell where only a school of porpoise, a minke whale and a Swedish freighter had intruded on the unusually placid seascape of the Minch, I sailed into the entrance of Loch Ewe, motored past the long, low Isle of Ewe and anchored close to a stone jetty off the village of Aultbea. It was nearly 8 p.m. and I was ravenous but, resisting the temptation to fill up on cheese sandwiches, I cooked a meal, set a table up in the cockpit and 'dined out' in style, watching the great red orb of the setting sun sinking towards the western horizon.

It was a gorgeously tranquil setting and difficult to imagine that Loch Ewe once thronged with shipping and sailors. In the 18th century, the minuscule village of Poolewe at the head of the loch was one of the major ports in the north-west of Scotland, and crossing the Minch I had sailed along the historic track of a regular mail service that once plied between Poolewe and Stornoway. On the return journey, cattle were brought over from Lewis and Harris and dumped in the sea to swim ashore before being driven over the hills to markets near Inverness.

Unlike most of the sea lochs in the Hebrides, which are cosily narrow, the mainland lochs on the east side of the Minch tend to be vast and wide, and during the Second World War were used extensively for all sorts of clandestine operations, and as a hidden base for the Royal Navy's fleet of battle ships.

Loch Ewe was the leaving point for the merchant ships that braved the Arctic convoys, though the quirk of geography that placed the loch on a latitude close to Moscow is an irony that might not have been fully appreciated by the crews, who faced appalling winter sea conditions to carry food and stores to the hungry Russians. With the emphasis of international sabre-rattling shifting from 'We've got a bigger battleship than you,' to 'We've got deadlier submarines,' Loch Ewe fitted nicely into the Admiralty's plans for a nationwide chain of nuclear submarine bases.

At the remote community of Mellon Charles, a name that could have been lifted from a twee village in the Surrey stockbroker belt, but apparently means 'little hill of Charles' in Gaelic, a gaunt collection of large Ministry of Defence sheds was surrounded by a fence and a lot of uneasy public speculation about what had been going on inside it. In keeping with the Admiralty tradition of having everything in duplicate, there was a Nato refuelling depot and submarine maintenance base only half a mile from where I was enjoying my meal in the evening sun, and I had an uncomfortable feeling that from one of the towers a steely-faced guard was monitoring my every move through binoculars, and dutifully noting down that I had greedily devoured four sausages, six new potatoes and a heap of mushy peas.

The ailing battery was still showing zero volts when I checked it, and hoisting an emergency paraffin anchor light into the rigging, I crawled into my sleeping bag and slept soundly until the skipper of a passing fishing boat thought it great fun to scare the wits out of me with a prolonged blast on his horn. Having spent a lot of my youth working on fishing boats, I can never understand why so many contemporary skippers seem to have a monumental chip on their shoulder about yachts, but I suppose the answer might lie in the enormous increase in the number of yachts that invade our coastal waters in the summer months and the arrogance of a minority of the new breed of sailors who handle them. In the event, the skipper had done me a favour; I had slept in and it was 9 a.m. and only two hours before the ebb that would carry me south.

14

DANGER OF EATING HEMLOCK –
THE PIRATE ISLAND – CALUM'S ROAD

Like many headlands in the west of Scotland, Rubha Réidh, separating Loch Ewe from my next destination, Loch Gairloch, ought to carry a health warning. The Admiralty Pilot described it as having heavy and dangerous seas extending several miles into the Minch, and Imray's *Yachtsman's Pilot* said very much the same, though they both qualified it by saying it was the result of wind against tide. When the foaming three-knot ebb gripped *Halcyon*'s keel and swept me along under the cliffs below the lighthouse, I heaved a sigh of relief that the previous day's light south-westerly had died away and it was flat calm. Under engine, I swished along at eight knots until Rubha Réidh was astern and the strength of the tidal stream gradually fell away.

The high-pressure system was certainly making its presence felt, with a vivid blue sky completely empty of clouds and a gentle sea that shimmered like a vat of molten sapphires. Rummaging in a locker, I unearthed the fishnet fridge and lowered it over the side with a cargo of cans of lager to cool ready for lunch, and at the same time streamed a fishing line over the stern. I was rewarded almost immediately with two fat mackerel, and while the autopilot kept me on course I grilled them on the cooker, and abeam of Longa Island which marked the entrance to Loch Gairloch, I stopped the engine and drifted in the sun, feasting on fresh mackerel washed down with chilled lager. No hotel in the world could have equalled it!

Entering Loch Gairloch, I made for Charlestown, a fish-landing harbour near the head of the loch, in the hope that there would be a chandler who would sell me a new battery, but there were so many fishing boats landing and departing at the quay, I knew I would be in the way if I tied up alongside, and I went across to the west side of the loch where the Pilot Book enthusiastically recommended a quiet inlet by Horrisdale Island. It was over a mile from the fish quay, but with the outboard on the dinghy I quickly zoomed back and found an obliging marine engineer who had the type of heavy duty battery I needed, but said it would take several hours to charge it and I would have to come back the following day.

In need of a few groceries, I strolled through the village until I found a shop. It was very small and seemed to be full of local ladies doing their weekly shopping, but they smiled sweetly and allowed me to squeeze past their ample bosoms and loaded baskets to reach for packs of bacon and sausages, cartons of long-life milk, boxes of eggs and loaves of bread.

Fancying a meal of prawns and scallops I had seen being unloaded from boats at the quay, I asked the shop assistant where I could buy some and was flabbergasted when she sniffed, 'You'll no be able to buy prawns in this village. The fishermen sell everything to the Spanish.' Shrewdly reading my thoughts, she went on, 'And you'll no be able to buy prawns straight off the boat either, they'll no let you have any. There is a fish van comes once a week from Aberdeen. You can order some if you wish.'

I could hardly believe I was in a Scottish fishing harbour being told I could not buy locally landed fish because it was being shipped abroad, and that a van came over a hundred miles from the east coast to sell fish to the locals. The engineer laughed when I went to his workshop and asked if it was true that the boats would not sell me any fish. 'Afraid so,' he said. 'The Spaniards have got the monopoly and say either they buy everything that's landed or they won't buy anything. It's crazy, I know, but that's the way it is.'

The anchorage by Eilean Horrisdale was wonderfully restful, and, snug in my sleeping bag, I read Martin Martin's account of his travels around the Western Isles in 1695. It was a fascinating insight into life on the islands at that time, and I winced in sympathy for Fergus Caird, who lived on the Isle of Skye and ate hemlock root thinking it was wild carrot; 'his eyes did presently roll about, the frame of his body was all in a strange convulsion and his pudenda retired so inwardly, that there was no discerning whether he had been male or female.'

I awoke to find the sun streaming through the hatch, and with two boiled eggs, a plateful of buttered toast and a pot of coffee, I lingered over breakfast in the cockpit, reluctant to break the spell of an incredibly lovely morning. I had told the engineer I would collect the battery at 10 a.m., and when I went across to his workshop he helped me carry it down to the stone steps of the quay and into the dinghy.

Back at *Halcyon*, getting it on board was a combination of juggling to stop the dinghy shooting away from under me while precariously balancing the battery on the after deck with one hand, and heaving on the tackle I had rigged on the mizzen mast for the outboard motor with the other. With the aid of a sheet of thick plywood I carried for emergency repairs, I eventually managed to slide it down the cabin steps and into the battery box under the pilot berth. It took only a few minutes to connect the cables and, hey presto, all the lights and the foghorn worked; the VHF radio, the GPS navigator, the Navtex (electronic navigation and weather message recorder) and the depth sounder came on, and BBC Radio Scotland boomed through the speakers.

Having to resort to basic navigation had been a useful memory-jogging exercise, but I was glad to have the electronic gadgets back. What to do with the dud battery was a problem – it was large and heavy, but conscience would not allow me to heave it over the side and I dragged it into the cockpit, where it stayed until I returned home to the Clyde.

About mid-afternoon I realised that a slothful life lying on deck in the sun was not going to get me down the coast to Loch Torridon, but *Halcyon* seemed as unwilling as I was to leave, and when I tried to crank the anchor in, it refused to let go of an obstruction on the bottom. Even when I retrieved the anchor buoy and hauled in the tripping line, the anchor remained stubbornly fast. I tried going ahead with the engine, then astern, but no luck, and I went back to cranking in the chain. I heaved and strained on the handle, expecting any minute that the winch would explode into a thousand pieces, but inch by painful inch the chain came in until the anchor reached the surface and I could see it was hooked onto a massive rusty chain that at some time had been a mooring.

With the boathook I coaxed the end of a spare piece of rope round the chain, and pulling it back on board tied the two ends together and hooked it round the samson post. With the winch slacked off, the anchor fell away from the chain and I hurriedly cranked it up and secured it to the stem head roller. All that was needed now was a sharp knife to cut the rope, and with a splash the chain sank back to its watery lair to lie in wait for another unsuspecting anchor. I was free, and within a couple of hours had cleared Loch Gairloch and motored down the coast to the headland of Red Point and the entrance to mighty Loch Torridon.

Some say that Loch Torridon is the most spectacular loch on the west coast of mainland Scotland, and when you sail in on a clear day and see the backdrop of sheer mountainsides bathed in the early evening sun, it certainly makes you stop and stare. The loch is made up of three sections, Loch Torridon, which narrows at its head and opens into Loch Shieldaig, which in turn opens up into Upper Loch Torridon. All together they add up to about twelve miles of landscape and lochscape that are overwhelmingly lovely, and in Loch Shieldaig most of the needs of the wandering sailor can be found in Shieldaig village, not least an inviting anchorage between the village and the Scots-pine-covered Shieldaig Island. I stayed there for two days exploring the island from the dinghy, taking a short walk into the hills and motoring *Halcyon* into Upper Loch Torridon, where I gaped in wonder at the scenery and overworked my camera taking endless shots of Liathach, the 1,055 metres of dramatic mountain magnificence that dwarfed the village of Torridon, lying at its feet.

The seaward end of Loch Torridon can be said to mark the southern extremity of the Minch, at least the eastern side of it, and thereafter it becomes a ten-mile-wide channel between the mainland and the enormous bulk of the Isle of Skye. This channel is itself divided into two individual sounds by the narrow elongated Island of Raasay, topped by the Island of Rona; on the west side is the Sound of Raasay and on the east side it is called the Inner Sound. For years the Royal Navy have used the Inner Sound for testing torpedoes and other equipment, and get very agitated when yachts bring their hush-hush activities to a grinding halt.

In 2002 wildlife conservationists became equally agitated when it was revealed that the Navy were testing a sonar device known to emit high-frequency soundwaves, which stranded, or in some cases killed, whales and dolphins and had been banned in the USA. It caused an uproar, but the Ministry of Defence put their flowery language department into gear and attempted to mollify the concerns of the objectors by issuing a statement reassuring them that 'a range of mitigating measures had been introduced to minimise the impact of sonar fitted to surface warships.'

By and large the amicable arrangement between the Navy and boat owners works well, though there are probably times when an enraged submarine commander longs to order 'Fire all torpedoes' and remove an offending sloop from the radar, but that would be bad for public relations, and the range control broadcasts regular bulletins on VHF about submarine activity in the hope that mariners will take heed. It was the Navy's morning broadcast that forced a change of plan when I sailed out of Loch Torridon with the intention of making my way down the Inner Sound to the unspoilt and picturesque anchorage of Plockton, in Loch Carron, some twenty miles to the south.

A darkening sky to the west was heralding the approach of another Atlantic low, and with plenty of leg-stretching walks ashore and sociable pubs where a sailor can take refuge from the weather behind an enjoyable pint, Plockton was the ideal bolt-hole. Unknown to me, the Admiralty had organised a 'friends of the UK' war game called a Nato exercise, and when a briskly efficient voice on VHF channel 8 advised all ships in the Inner Sound to keep clear, I decided on the longer 'scenic route' round the top of the Island of Rona and down the Sound of Raasay.

With scores of tiny islands, hidden inlets and inviting anchorages bristling with submerged rocks that feed on yacht keels, Rona is typically Hebridean in character. About four miles long by perhaps a mile at its widest, the island is isolated from its near neighbour Raasay by the fast-flowing tidal waterway of Caol Rona, and with a sprinkling of hills handy as lookouts, it once had an evil reputation as the home of pirates who raided ships passing through the sounds.

As I once discovered when a Navy patrol boat smartly escorted me out of it because they needed it cleared for a special exercise, the Admiralty have taken over Loch a' Bhraige, a wide and easily approachable inlet at the north end of Rona, and are not keen on visitors. The welcome, however, is very different at the south end of the island, where the old pirate base of Acairsaid Mhor (the big harbour) is the kind of yacht anchorage that lingers in the memory, and the Danish lady owner of the island has invested a lot of time and money in improving landing facilities.

It was low water when I arrived, which helped to avoid the approach hazards, and keeping well away from a rocky reef near the jetty I let go the anchor in a two-metre pool. The cloud that had been gathering in the west during the day seemed to have stalled over the Outer Hebrides, and BBC Radio Scotland's evening forecaster said that there would be at least one more day of sun and blue sky before strong wind and rain charged in from the Atlantic. Taking advantage of the clear visibility that often signals the approach of rain, I rowed ashore with my cameras to climb Meall Acarsaid, at 123 metres the island's highest hill, and marvel at the commanding view the pirates of old had of both of the Sounds, the mountains of Torridon, the coast of Skye and, in the far distance, the island of Lewis.

There are few places in the British Isles to match the west of Scotland and the Hebrides for clear skies and breathtakingly spectacular sunsets, and I watched spellbound as the blood-red sun sank slowly towards the sea, turning it into burnished gold. A musician could have matched notes and instruments to the ever changing colours of pinks, reds, browns and blacks in the sky, and written a full orchestral score with a final bursting crescendo when the sun finally plunged below the western horizon and day turned to night.

The earth had spun round on its axis while I was asleep, and when shafts of sunlight streaming through the skylight got me out of my bunk to switch the anchor light off, a crimson sun was already rising steadily in the east. It was the weather portent that warned a red sky in the morning is a sailor's warning, but while I was having breakfast the soothing voice of the weather lady on BBC Radio Scotland said the old rhymes should not be taken too seriously and promised a fine, sunny day with a light westerly wind.

It was a perfect day for exploring Rona, and I went ashore and called at Rona Lodge to ask Bill Cowie, the manager, if I could wander over the island. There is no law of trespass in Scotland and, within reason, walkers can go anywhere; but on the occupied privately-owned islands it is a useful courtesy to ask permission to land from the owner or the manager, who in the majority of cases will be welcoming and helpful. Bill Cowie was the laid back 'nothing is too much trouble' breed of

Church Cave and stone pews, Rona

manager, who spread a map out and said if I wanted to see something that was probably unique in the whole of the UK I should visit Church Cave on the east side of the island, and pointed out where it was.

In his *Description of the Western Islands of Scotland*, Martin Martin dismisses Rona as 'the most unequal rocky piece of ground to be seen anywhere . . . the whole is covered with long heath', but since his visit in the 17th century a few changes have been made. Bulldozed tracks and worn footpaths have made it easier to get around, but the tortuous path to Church Cave must have had many a parishioner, particularly the elderly, wondering if there was a less strenuous way of guaranteeing eternal salvation.

The path followed a winding route through bog, rock and heather until it dipped down a steep, stony scramble by the side of a cliff to an arched entrance like that of a great cathedral, and inside was one of the most intriguing arrangements of stones I had ever seen. For centuries it had been the place of worship of the islanders, and inside there was a stone pillar used as a lectern, flat stones in rows like pews and, most captivating of all, a stone depression used as a baptismal font cleverly placed under drips from the cave roof that provided the water.

Even after a church was built on the west side of Rona in the 1900s, the island mothers were still prepared to brave the tough slog to have their babies baptised in the cave, and from its airy location looking down on the Inner Sound, it did not test the imagination very much to picture the congregation struggling to hear the service when the cave was being blasted by torrential rain and a fierce winter gale.

Leaving the cave and climbing the low hills in the north of the island, I could see that the bank of black cloud that had hung over Lewis was on the move again; and by the time I had returned to the boat landing, it had devoured the sun and transformed the bright sunlit haven of Acarsaid Mhor into a sullen, grey, windswept lagoon with angry white caps churning the water. The depression had arrived, and by early evening the wind was blowing hard from the west and it was raining. By midnight it had backed to the south and was blowing straight into the haven and, fearing that I would drag anchor in the soft mud of the bottom, I lowered the angel down the chain, but the respite was only temporary.

At 5 a.m. the wailing of the anchor alarm got me out of my bunk with a rush, and I shot into the cockpit in time to start the engine and save *Halcyon* from being driven onto the rocky reef. Twice I dropped the anchor in a fresh place and each time the wind blew me back towards the reef. There was no alternative sheltering place in Acarsaid Mhor from the violent southerly, so I winched the anchor up and motored out into Raasay Sound and headed for the island of Fladday, close to Raasay, where I knew I would find shelter.

Butting into the seas it was a very uncomfortable three miles and took over an hour, but it was worth it. Tucked in between Fladday and Raasay, the wind hardly rippled the surface when I lit the cooker to prepare a delayed breakfast, while overhead it roared like a demon. I was pinned down behind Fladday for two days, but it was no hardship. It gave me the opportunity to go ashore and visit the famous 'Calum's Road'.

While on a walking holiday on Raasay in the 1970s I met a man repairing the rough, unsurfaced track between Arnish and Brochel, two isolated settlements close to Fladday Island, and we chatted for a while. Years later I was astonished to learn that, more than repairing it the man, Calum MacLeod from Arnish, was actually building it single-handed, all one and three-quarter miles of it, because the County Council had consistently refused to extend the surfaced road that ran from the ferry terminal in the south of the island to Brochel and so reduce the hardship of the crofters of Arnish and beyond. They had to carry all their needs along a narrow track that climbed, dipped, turned and twisted, traversing high along the edge of Loch Arnish for nearly two miles.

Tired of waiting for the bureaucrats, Calum launched into the job himself, and with only a pick, a shovel and a wheelbarrow, and incredible resilience and determination, dug his way uphill and downhill for over ten years. In recognition of his awe-inspiring achievement, he was awarded the British Empire Medal, and had a song and a book written about him, but it was in 1982 that he was presented with the ultimate recognition of his work. The County Council finally adopted his road and gave it a coating of tarmac!

The gale met me with full ferocity and it had started to rain when I climbed up from the Fladday anchorage, and though I eventually reached Calum's Road it was too exhausting to walk into the wind, so to make the most of the day ashore I turned and followed a thin path that went for miles through rough bogland until it reached the very tip of Raasay and looked across to a wet and windy Rona. It was only later that I read in Haswell-Smith's *The Scottish Islands* that, as well as building his road, Calum had also been the local postman, and having collected the mail at Brochel he walked to the tip of Raasay, rowed across to Rona, walked the length of Rona to the lighthouse to deliver the mail, then retraced his steps. A total of twenty-one miles.

I bought a few prawns off the skipper of a small fishing boat that came alongside when I got back to *Halcyon*, and when I mentioned Calum he said, 'Aye, they've lost the mould that sort of laddie was made out of.'

15

THE FILM-MAKER'S CASTLE – GAVIN MAXWELL – ARISAIG SKINNY DIPPERS

During my second night of pleasant captivity behind Eilean Fladday, the wind died away to a breeze and, though the land blanked out the morning broadcasts of the BBC and Stornoway Coastguard, I was cheered by the barometer having risen a few notches. There was no reason for staying any longer, and after breakfast I raised anchor and sailed into Raasay Sound. My food was running low and the nearest shops were in Portree on Skye. But as I wanted to top up my water tanks as well, to continue to Kyle of Lochalsh, where there was a visitors' pontoon with fresh water and shops only a short walk away, was the obvious answer.

The light wind had gone round to the north and I goosewinged down the coast of Raasay, followed by a most enjoyable reach between the islands of Scalpay, Longay and Pabay and under the wide span of the modern concrete bridge, which many argue has robbed Skye of its island status.

At Kyle of Lochalsh I found a berth on the pontoon immediately astern of an enormous sloop that had a gleaming aluminium mast the height of a factory chimney, and a uniformed crew with lots of gold braid who were not disposed to return the cheery greeting of the underling in the wooden gaff yawl who had tied up close to them. Twenty-two nautical miles in three and a half hours was not at all bad for a heavy boat not noted for its speed under sail, though the spring ebb might have had something to do with it.

In Gaelic, Kyle means the same as Caol – a sound or a narrow passage of water – and there was a time when Kyle of Lochalsh was one of the most important rail and ferry terminals on the west coast of Scotland. Sadly, progress, that excuse for change, threatened its life blood in 1972 when a shorter and more economical route was chosen for the ferry from Stornoway to the mainland, and then in the 1990s, when the residents of Skye complained that going 'over the sea to Skye' was all very romantic in song but was quicker by car, and campaigned for a bridge to replace the Kyle of Lochalsh ferries.

The railway operators, accustomed to coping with swarms of passengers travelling to and from Lewis and Skye, soon found they had reduced to a trickle, and trimmed their timetables accordingly. Sages had shaken their heads and prophesied that, having lost the rail and ferry trade, the town would wither and die.

I went ashore expecting to see a ghost town of boarded up shops and empty streets, but instead cafes and shops were bursting with tourists and the car park was full to overflowing. The whole place looked as if it had been newly painted, and sailors were particularly well catered for with well-stocked shops, water available at the pontoon, fuel at the commercial dock, a row of moorings and a spotlessly clean toilet block with hot showers.

Returning to *Halcyon* loaded with food and vital liquid – a bottle of malt whisky for me and a container of paraffin for the cooking stove – I realised it was almost low water and too late to take the tide through Kyle Rhea narrows into the Sound of Sleat. With a spring rate of eight knots, there was only one way a small boat could go and that was with it.

Loch Duich Anchorage and Eilean Donan Castle

There was no possibility of going through the narrows until the following day, and with wind forecast to go back to the south, I cast off from the pontoon and sailed through Loch Alsh and down to Loch Duich and the enjoyable little bay of Totaig. Barely a dent on the chart, it is a perfect anchorage for winds south of west or east, and on one occasion I rode out a southerly force nine and, apart from the noise, was hardly aware of it.

Totaig has its disadvantages, though, not least a large drying rock taking up the best part of the anchorage, and a playfully gyrating tide that runs strongly clockwise on the flood and equally strongly anticlockwise with the ebb – and woe betide anyone whose anchor is not well bedded in – but what a super view there is of Eilean Donan Castle less than half a mile away on the opposite side of the loch.

Said to be the most photographed castle in Scotland and pictured on thousands of calendars and boxes of shortbread, it is the kind of setting that film-makers rave about, and great names like Errol Flynn in *The Master of Ballantrae* and David Niven in *Bonnie Prince Charlie* have clambered over the castle walls; the New Avengers with Patrick Macnee and Joanna Lumley have done some avenging at Eilean Donan, and it was from the castle that Pierce Brosnan saved the world in the Bond movie *The World is Not Enough*. Whichever angle it was viewed from, the superb castle fitted naturally into the Highland landscape and could have graced any film from *The Sound of Music* to *Dracula*.

When it had gone dark and I was relaxing in the cockpit with a glass of Spey-side malt, the castle was silhouetted in a blaze of orange floodlights, and wisps of mist rising off the surface of the loch were swirling eerily around the walls. It was as though some movie mogul was building a film set for a gruesome epic of 'the Scottish play', *Macbeth*, with murderous wives and witches crawling all over the place.

According to the BBC's morning weather forecaster, anywhere between the north of Skye and the Torridon hills was the dividing line between the fickle Atlantic low-pressure systems that had been coming and going across the Minch and an area of settled weather that was lying over the rest of Scotland. It was also roughly the southern limit of Stornoway Coastguard's operational area, and it was from Clyde Coastguard's morning forecast that I got the news that good weather was on the way.

As if to confirm it, a bright sun burnt a hole in the clouds, and by the time I had left Totaig and was dodging about at the entrance to Kyle Rhea waiting for the ebb to flow south, it was warm enough to remind me it was still summer. Going through Kyle Rhea in a boat with a spring ebb under it has been likened to a turd being flushed down a lavatory, and while the description may be vulgar, the experience proves it very apt.

In the 1890s, aboard the Free Church yacht *Betsey*, used for taking visiting ministers to remote communities, Hugh Miller wrote, 'Never . . . have I seen such a tide. It danced and wheeled and came boiling in huge masses from the bottom; and now our bows heaved abruptly round in one direction, and now they jerked as suddenly round in another, and though there blew a moderate breeze at the time, the helm failed to keep the sails steadily full . . . [O]n we swept in the tideway like a cork caught during a thunder shower in the rapids of the High Street.'

Large ships are just as powerless, and a caution in the Admiralty Pilot states, '[T]he ship slewed violently to port through an arc of 70°. Later, at the other end of the Kyle . . . when steaming with revolutions for nearly 12kn, no headway was made relative to the land.'

The skipper of the little car ferry that plied across the sound where the tide is at its strongest was used to seeing yachts being flushed past him, often sideways or stern first, and very considerately went round *Halcyon* in a wide arc while I fought with the tiller to keep in a straight line. Escaping from the clutches of a violent eddy that spun *Halcyon* round through 360°, we were finally decanted into Glenelg Bay and I steered for Sandaig Island lighthouse, four miles down the Sound of Sleat.

I had a particular reason for wanting to anchor and go ashore in Sandaig Bay close to the lighthouse. In the mid-1950s, I forget the precise year, I had walked over the hills to Sandaig from Shiel Bridge on Loch Duich and came down to a shepherd's cottage where the occupant was clearly not pleased to see me and, unlike Highland shepherds of the time, most inhospitable. But when he spoke it was obvious he was no shepherd, and apologising for intruding on his solitude I went away.

It was only when I read the book *Ring of Bright Water* that I realised the cottage was the one immortalised as Camusfearna, and the man who had ordered me to 'clear off' was the author Gavin Maxwell. He told me in no uncertain words that he detested hikers and campers, and I sympathised. His cottage was set in one of the most delightful locations on earth, and he wanted it to himself. But how the passage of time can change a landscape almost beyond recognition!

When I rowed ashore in Sandaig Bay, the cottage had gone and the fields around it were overpowered by a colossal plantation of spruce. The only reminder of Gavin Maxwell and the inspiration for his heart-warming book was a plaque on the ground where Camusfearna had stood, and the author's ashes buried underneath it. A poignant epitaph on the plaque to Edal, an otter who died in the fire that had destroyed Camusfearna in 1968, read, 'Whatever joy she gave to you, give back to nature.' If only that were possible!

With the tide under me and a light westerly breeze filling the sails, I made good time along the Sound of Sleat between the Isle of Skye on the west side and the wild coast of Knoydart to the east, and I passed the wide entrance of Loch Hourn (the loch of hell) and Isle Ornsay on Skye. It was from Isle Ornsay that many of the distraught Knoydart crofters were transported to Canada during the Highland Clearances of the 19th century.

I had hoped to spend a few nights in Mallaig harbour, but when I approached the entrance I could sense it had obviously been a successful day for the fishing fleet and boats were steaming in at full speed to be first to unload their catch. Knowing there would be little room for a yacht, and even less of a welcome in the overcrowded docks, I turned away for Arisaig, eight miles to the south, and was glad I did.

A few miles beyond Mallaig, two enormous basking sharks came close to *Halcyon*, their great mouths wide open as they swallowed millions of microscopic plankton. The survival of these harmless creatures is causing a lot of concern among conservationists and many point the finger of blame at Gavin Maxwell. In 1946 he started a shark-fishing venture with a partner, 'Tex' Geddes, from Soay, an island between Rum and Skye. It resulted in a serious decline in the number of basking sharks on the west coast, and scientists say they have never really recovered. The increasing pollution of the sea has not helped and to be fair to Maxwell, in the austere post-war years of the 1940s the nation's priority was food, and conservation was not the war cry it is today.

Hardly had my friendly sharks sunk below the surface when a minke whale swam astern of *Halcyon*, blowing and snorting, and I spent so much time trying to photograph it that the tide had turned when I entered the tortuous channel leading to Arisaig, and it needed the full power of the engine to push against the ebb.

The tiny village of Arisaig spreads out around the head of an eye-catching and reasonably sheltered haven called Loch nan Ceall, which was relatively unknown until a confusing arrangement of marker beacons that marked the zigzag approach was sorted out to something akin to the international buoyage system, and then its popularity with west coast cruising addicts increased enormously. Keen to spend a day walking the hills above the village, I hired a mooring from the local boatyard to save me the fear of finding that *Halcyon* had dragged anchor while I was away.

'You'll find there is a path starts just by the railway station,' said a helpful man in the boatyard when I enquired how I could get to the hills. The railway station was really no more than two platforms and a signal box that appeared to serve as a popular meeting place for a flock of gulls which, helped along by the strident squawkings of a few oystercatchers, were having a very noisy meeting on the roof. I hoped they were protesting about inconsiderate boat crews who dumped plastic bottles and other non-biodegradable rubbish into the sea, but I knew there was nothing they could do about the relentless poisoning of their watery world any more than I could.

The path was exactly where the boatyard man said it would be, and I followed it through a throng of sweet-smelling wild flowers and broad-leaved fern. The air was warm, wild bees were humming from flower to flower, and delicate red admiral butterflies were perched on stems of bracken, their fragile wings spread out in the sun.

It was a day that erased from the mind the anguish of howling winds, scary overfalls, tide rips, submerged rocks and dragging anchors; and I climbed higher up the hill and looked across the Sound of Sleat to the islands of Rum, Eigg and Muck floating on an azure sea. In the distance were the saw-toothed ridges of the Cuillins of Skye and there was no doubt in my mind that in spite of its sometimes tedious and changeable weather, the west of Scotland had few equals for adventurous and enjoyable sailing.

My objective was a hill called Carn a' Mhadaidh-ruaidh which, with my poor knowledge of Gaelic, I guessed meant the Cairn of the Red Fox or Dog. Rising 503 metres above Arisaig, it was hardly Ben Nevis but it was still a long uphill slog over rough, wet ground, first having to overcome a 351 metre grassy peak then one of 394 metres that dropped steeply from its summit to a small loch at the foot of the final climb.

The sun was high in the sky and I was making for the loch to fill my water bottle when I heard voices, and was shocked to see two completely naked women sitting on a rock like a pair of mermaids. When they saw me they shrieked with laughter and covered their well-formed bodies, and my embarrassment, by leaping into the water up to their necks. With a feeble wave of apology I hurried by, not daring to look back until I was well out of sight. My heart was thumping when I reached the summit of Carn a' Mhadaidh-ruaidh and it was not all to do with the steep climb.

The view in every direction was absolutely magnificent. As well as the seascape of islands to the west I had a clear view of Loch Morar to the north, at 310 metres the deepest expanse of freshwater in the UK.

To the south of Arisaig was Loch nan Uamh (nan oo-a) the place where, after his flight from the Culloden battlefield across the Highlands, and with the help of brave Flora MacDonald via the Hebrides, the dream of Prince Charles Edward Louis John Casimir Severino Maria Stuart – Bonnie Prince Charlie – to regain the throne of Britain finally ended when, on 20 September 1746, he climbed aboard a French ship and sailed away from Scotland, never to return.

Below the east side of the summit I could see a stalker's track snaking down the hill, and I followed it down a long steep-sided glen to the main road. The map showed a track leading to Arisaig that fortunately saved me the ordeal of tramping along miles of vehicle-choked tarmac, and I reached the village shop gasping with thirst and sat in the sun with a large ice cream, celebrating the end of a wonderfully enjoyable ten-mile walk.

16

ARDNAMURCHAN POINT – THE OFFICERS' MESS – TWO VERY FINE GENTLEMEN

When I left Arisaig it was dry but overcast and flat calm, and under engine I set a course for Ardnamurchan Point, fifteen miles to the south and the most westerly point on mainland Britain. While *Halcyon* steered herself with the aid of the autopilot, it was an ideal chance to catch up on a few 'make do and mend' jobs, like screwing two clips on deck to hold the anchor-winch handle, splicing new eyes into the tackles controlling the backstays, and repairing the staysail. While lashed along the guardrails on the foredeck, it had become involved in a relationship with the spare anchor, and the rubbing motion had worn several small holes in the sailcloth. Cutting the patches from a spare piece of cloth, I first glued them on both sides of the holes, then put stitches in. Jeckells of Wroxham, who had made all *Halcyon*'s sails, might have thrown up their hands in disgust but I was quite proud of the finished job.

Sitting on the foredeck and leaning back against the mast while *Halcyon* gently pitched and rolled was pleasantly relaxing, and as Ardnamurchan Point and the grey granite tower of the lighthouse drew ever closer, my mind went back to when I was a keeper there after being transferred from the Butt of Lewis. There was a shortage of lighthouse keepers at the time, and for a while there was only a Principal Keeper and myself working watches of four hours on and four hours off, round the clock, seven days a week, and it was devilishly wearying.

Even when I got married, the stuffed shirts who ran the Northern Lighthouse Board in the early 1960s would not let me have more than few days off, and I had my honeymoon at the lighthouse. But I was still on duty, and the marriage was only just consummated when I had to leap out of bed and race up the tower to wind up the mechanism that kept the lantern revolving.

Despite the hardships, it was an enjoyable life and sheer luxury compared to the hell of working on trawlers. As *Halcyon* surged past the now automated lighthouse in a rolling swell the Point had an evil reputation for, I was overcome with nostalgia and, pouring a small dram of whisky into a mug, I raised a toast to the memory of all lighthouse keepers and to the happy times I had enjoyed at Ardnamurchan Point.

Ardnamurchan lighthouse – the most westerly point on mainland Britain

There is some dispute about the Gaelic name of Ardnamurchan Point. Some say it is Ard na Murchan (the hill of the great sea). On the other hand, the Northern Lighthouse Board says the two most likely names are Aird Muirchu (the point of the seahounds or otters) and Aird Muirchol (the point of the pirates or wreckers). Whichever one is favoured, what is indisputable is that the Point marks the entrance to the Sound of Mull, a long and sometimes boisterous stretch of water, beloved by coasters for its sheltered passage and by divers for its diverse range of historic wrecks. Above all, it is synonymous with Tobermory, quite possibly the most popular watering hole for yacht crews anywhere in Scotland. Its pubs are legendary, its restaurants hard to beat, and its shops and mooring facilities are everything cruising men or women could ask for.

On the downside, Tobermory can be crowded and noisy and for that reason I usually avoided it, but I was desperately short of methylated spirits for lighting my paraffin cooker and on Tobermory sea front was a chandlers that sold it. Locating a vacant visitors' mooring among the forest of masts packed into the harbour was not easy, and I was on my third circuit when a yacht ahead of me suddenly cast off and put to sea, and I pounced on the mooring buoy and hauled it aboard.

When I rowed ashore, the chandlers was closed and a card in the door said 'Back in an hour'. Coachloads of tourists were streaming from the car park and the sea front was jammed with people, so I retreated onto the tiny beach and fell into conversation with a retired history professor who was busy taking photographs of the old fish quay for a book he was writing about Mull. He insisted on bombarding me with facts, saying it was the third largest island in the west of Scotland, was twenty-four miles long from north to south and twenty-six miles from east to west, had something in the region of three hundred miles of coastline and was once a volcano.

It was all interesting stuff, but a mouth-watering aroma wafting from the fish quay was distracting me and I was glad when he went to take photographs of a fishing boat coming in and I was able to join a queue in front of a van. The professor had gone when I finished my lunch, but I could usefully have contributed to his statistical account of Mull by letting him know that a bag of Tobermory fish and chips was large, hot and utterly delicious.

I called in at the local Co-op for a few groceries, bought a large haggis from a butcher, got four bottles of meths from the chandlers and rowed back to *Halcyon*. I was looking forward to a mug of coffee before I set off again, but a race from Oban had just ended at the harbour and the crews were rowdily rafting up on moorings. It was time to leave.

An easterly breeze had sprung up but it was 'on the nose' and the prospect of beating back and forth down the narrow Sound of Mull for several hours had no appeal. Long past the age when I revelled in long thrashes to windward, boating for me was the pleasure of visiting new anchorages and harbours. If the wind was fair the sails were hoisted; if it wasn't then I used the engine, and it was the trusty Volvo diesel that pushed *Halcyon* down the fifteen nautical miles from Tobermory to Craignure, the ferry terminal for Mull, at the eastern end of the Sound.

I had been looking forward to spending a peaceful night on a visitors' mooring in Craignure Bay, and was deeply disappointed to discover that they had been removed. It had been a long day; I was tired and was preparing to let go the anchor when the wind backed to the north and stirred up a lively sea in the bay. An uncomfortable night rolling and pitching was not what I wanted and, aware that I would be very close to a lee shore, I thumbed through the tide table in Reeds Almanac and saw I still had time to get in behind Craignure's old stone quay before it dried out.

There was a small open fishing boat tied up ahead of me when I went alongside the rough stone wall, but the owner was aboard and obligingly moved forward to give *Halcyon* plenty of room to lie against it. With the anchor chain ranged along the port side deck, and with the weight of two anchors and four containers of diesel on top of it, *Halcyon* had a nice cant into the wall and, protected by every fender I could muster, sank down with ebbing tide and dried out on an even keel. My friendly fisherman helped me to secure the warps, and when I asked what had happened to the moorings he said not enough yachts had been using them to justify the cost of maintenance, and the local mooring association had lifted them.

I was asleep when the tide came in again and floated *Halcyon* about 11 p.m. though, apart from a few groans from the warps and an occasional thump against the wall caused by the swell, she hardly moved and I slept undisturbed until 8 a.m. *Halcyon* had dried out again, and although the wind still blew from the north it was very light and a rapidly rising sun bathed Craignure Bay in a warm glow. I climbed up onto the quay with a mug of coffee and sat on a bollard admiring the lovely island of Mull, which Dr Johnson, on his tour of the Hebrides in 1773, unfairly described as 'a most dolorous country'.

With the rocks exposed, the aroma of bladder wrack ('the tangle of the isles') hung heavily in the air, and on the opposite side of the Sound the hills of Morvern floated in a purple haze. I was only a lad when I first visited Mull in a fishing boat in the early 1950s, and a choir, welcoming a visiting dignitary who had arrived aboard a Royal Navy ship, was standing on Craignure's stone quay singing the island's 'national anthem' in Gaelic:

> *The Isle of Mull is of Isles the fairest,*
> *Of ocean's gems 'tis the first and rarest;*
> *Green grassy island of sparkling fountains,*
> *Of waving woods and high tow'ring mountains.*

A homesick Dugald MacPhail had penned the song a century before while working away from home in England, and listening to the haunting sound sent a tingle down my back. To me, as an impressionable youth staring open-mouthed at the lovely Highland girls in the choir, it represented everything that was romantic about island life, but the idyllic land portrayed in MacPhail's poem has changed. Perhaps more than any other Scottish island its native population has been thinned down by incomers, and so many retired military types have chosen to end their days on the 'green grassy island' it has been dubbed 'the Officers' Mess'.

The MacBrayne car ferry *Isle of Mull* swept into the bay while I was finishing off my coffee and, helped by all the electronic gadgets invented to assist mariners to manoeuvre their ships, the anonymous captain on the bridge brought it neatly alongside the new 'roll on, roll off' pier. The hundreds of holidaymakers jostling to get ashore probably never gave him a thought, though there was a time when MacBrayne captains were noted for their seamanship and Highland humour. Hughie Carmichael, the skipper of a cargo boat that used to operate out of Craignure, once told me an amusing story involving Lady MacLean from Duart Castle. Before the new pier at Craignure was built, the steamers had to land passengers at the old stone quay by rowing boat, a task notoriously difficult in rough seas; and one day when the ship arrived the weather was so bad the captain was reluctant to risk it, but the only passenger for Craignure, Lady MacLean of Duart Castle, pleaded with him to try. By clever seamanship he eventually managed to bring his ship alongside the rowing boat and Lady MacLean was unceremoniously dumped in. As the ship hurriedly steamed away she called out, 'Thank you for your help, Captain, and for the help of God.'

'Aye m'lady,' shouted the captain, 'two very fine gentlemen.'

17

ISLAND RAILWAY – JACOBITE-INSPIRED WITCHCRAFT

'And where will you be making for today?' said a Highland voice. I had finished breakfast and was busy taking advantage of *Halcyon* being dried out to scrub the hull and remove numerous clinging barnacles that had developed a taste for my expensive antifouling. I looked up to see my fisherman friend smiling down at me from the quay.

'I've nothing planned,' I said. 'In fact, if I'm not in the way I'd like to stay another night and maybe go for a walk on the hills.'

'Och, you'll be fine there,' he laughed. 'The yachters are more used to picking up a mooring in Tobermory than drying out against a quay wall. I'll keep an eye on your boat while you are away.' He turned to go, then stopped. 'If you want to see something interesting why don't you take a run on our wee railway to Torosay Castle; it's the only passenger railway in all of the islands.' Then pointing to a headland near the quay, 'The station is just over there.'

I thanked him for his help and went back to scrubbing the hull. Trains were not something I was particularly interested in, I preferred a hill walk; but the more I thought about it the more it appealed. I always enjoyed seeking out new experiences on my travels, and if this was the only passenger railway anywhere on the islands I should take a ride on it.

The story of the founding of the Mull and West Highland Narrow Gauge Railway Company Limited, a name almost as long as the line, is fascinating, and started way back in 1858 when the Guthrie family built Torosay Castle on the edge of Craignure. The then owner started to construct a drive from the castle to the old quay, but when it reached a point where it had to go through land owned by the church, the minister refused permission and the drive was abandoned and became totally overgrown.

Fast-forward 120 years, and the present owner of Torosay, David Guthrie-James, an ex-naval officer who had distinguished himself during the Second World War by escaping from a German prisoner of war camp, put his tunnelling skills to good use at home by crawling on his stomach for half a mile through the jungle of overgrown track with a view to converting the old drive into a railway line to carry tourists from Craignure to visit his house, garden and teashop.

It took years of frustrations and unpaid hard graft by volunteers before finally the line was officially opened in 1984. It was at the single-platform Craignure station that I boarded, or rather wedged myself into, one of three Lilliputian coaches crammed with excited youngsters and worried teachers frantically trying to count their charges. Hauled by a miniature engine, the little train puffed and wheezed its way above the shore of the Sound, and I caught snatches of views across sea and mountains, even to far-away Ben Nevis, before it plunged through sparkling woodland flanked by hedgerows filled with wild flowers.

It was a delightful journey of nearly two miles, though for a reason not revealed in the railway company's leaflet, the terminal at Torosay station stopped short of the Castle by a quarter of a mile. Reaching the door of the castle, really no more than a large country house, I was peeved to find it closed for the day, but the maze of woodland paths and shrubs in the grounds were a blaze of colour and I spent an hour running amok with my camera.

Miniature railways anywhere in the world are invariably run by volunteers who bubble with enthusiasm; and while waiting for the train back to Craignure, an elderly chap sporting a railwayman's peaked cap insisted on giving me a tour of the maintenance sheds. He was bursting with information about the size and power of the locomotives, but when I asked why the line had not been taken to Torosay Castle, and perhaps even extended round the adjoining bay to the MacLean stronghold of Duart Castle, he suddenly had an urgent job to attend to, and I wondered if I might have ventured onto the thin ice of local politics.

The school party arrived and noisily swarmed into the coaches while the teachers tried their best to do a head count, and shouted above the racket asking anxiously if anyone had seen Morag and Fiona. Reluctant to be branded a killjoy, I kept it to myself that after the railway man had left me I had seen his teenage assistant locked into what appeared to be a passionate form of mouth-to-mouth resuscitation with Morag, or it might have been Fiona, behind the engine shed.

The search for the girls was reaching hysteria pitch and I was about to reveal all when they suddenly appeared, explaining that they had been answering a call of nature, which was true, but it was a different call from the one the teachers had in mind. They were pulled into a carriage by their giggling mates, and with a blast on the whistle and much laboured 'chuffing' from its funnel, the little engine heaved and strained and the coaches slowly gathered speed on their return trip to Craignure station.

When the train emerged from the shelter of the woodland a sudden gust of wind rocked the carriages, and I was concerned to see that it had veered north-east and increased from a light breeze to a squally force six, and nasty white-capped rollers were sweeping into the bay. It was high water, and when the train stopped I ran for the quay and was horrified to see that *Halcyon* was crashing against the wall in the swell. My fisherman friend had already arrived and was pulling his boat to safety.

'I'm going to leave and go across to Eilean Ridire on Morvern,' I shouted. 'Will you cast me off?'

'Aye, you're doing the right thing,' he shouted back. 'Just be careful when you get past the end of the quay, the seas will push you sideways. Start your engine.'

Untying the mooring warps he flung them on deck, and with the engine at full throttle *Halcyon* surged forward and away from the quay. Immediately a big sea crashed into the bow and slewed it round, and we were heading straight for a foaming mass of rocks. I was sure we would be smashed to pieces, but with the helm hard over *Halcyon* slowly turned into the wind and started to pull forward.

Ahead the sea was completely white, as if someone had poured millions of tons of soap powder into it and, knowing I was in for a rough ride, I pulled a lifejacket on and clipped a lifeline onto the cockpit fitting. With the tiller on autopilot I managed to stow the mooring warps and pull the fenders aboard, but the sea was so wild I could do no more than dump them on the side decks and rush back before the next roller swept along the decks and boiled over the stern.

The anchorage of Eilean Ridire was a tiny island tucked in against the Morvern coast, almost opposite Craignure and well sheltered from a north-easterly wind, but first I had to cross an expanse of water infamous for its tidal overfalls and swirl-ing eddies.

When the torrent of water pouring out of the twenty-eight-mile-long Loch Linnhe collides with the tide flowing out of the twenty-mile-long Sound of Mull, the result can be, and often is, a spectacular maelstrom of angry seas, and never before had *Halcyon*'s self-draining cockpit been tested as much as it was on that crossing. I seemed to be constantly up to my knees in water. The wind had increased, but what it was on the Beaufort Scale I could only guess; it caused wave after wave to break over the deck, first on the port side, then the starboard and even over the stern, but stoutly built *Halcyon* weathered the lot and eventually, battered, bruised and soaking wet, I dropped anchor behind Eilean Rubha an Ridire and poured myself a large dram. It had taken ninety minutes to travel three miles.

Well protected from the wind by the high coast of Morvern, there was only a light breeze wafting around the island, but it was unseasonably chilly and I coaxed life into the charcoal-burning stove to warm the cabin. While I prepared my evening meal, the burners on the cooker boosted the cabin heat even higher, and surrounded by drying clothes and dripping oilskins I sat down to a meal of haggis, potatoes and hot coffee, wallowing in a cosy fug while out in the Sound the wind screamed like a thousand banshees. Clyde Coastguard said the wind would moderate but that the outlook was unsettled with further low systems blowing in from the Atlantic.

Scotland's summer weather pattern seemed to have turned on its head. At the Butt of Lewis lighthouse, and later at Ardnamurchan Point, I was responsible for compiling the weather reports used in the shipping forecasts. Rarely were there more than two or three short gales during the summer months, and the wind seldom blew harder than force three or four. Now, strong winds and rain throughout the summer were becoming the norm and I could sympathise with a disgruntled American who once said to me, 'The only time you can tell it's summer in the UK is when the doggone rain gets warmer.'

The morning dawned grey and overcast but the Coastguards were right, the wind had faded to a moderate breeze and the sea looked less threatening. Inflating the dinghy, I rowed across to the island to photograph a flock of eider duck who were making their funny ooh-ing sound, like a gathering of old ladies exchanging titbits of juicy gossip. The rocky crevices were jammed with old fishing net, lobster pot buoys and the battered remains of a small fibreglass motorboat, a reminder that Eilean Rubha an Ridire (island of the promontory of the knight), my safe haven from the gale, was also renowned for wrecking a ship that lay only a few metres from where I was anchored.

In 1690 a Royal Navy frigate, the *Dartmouth*, was engaged in subduing Jacobite sympathisers in the Sound of Mull and on 9 October was anchored below Duart Castle, the home of the MacLeans, who were staunch supporters of the Jacobite cause, when 'with Jacobite-inspired witchcraft' it dragged its anchor in a storm. It drifted across to Rubha an Ridire where, 'to the great rejoicing of the MacLeans', it hit a reef and sank with the loss of its captain and all but six of the crew.

It was a site of rich pickings for divers and souvenir hunters until officialdom moved into action and declared the *Dartmouth* a protected wreck.

The island was also the scene of the wacky loss of two steam puffers (the traditional small Scottish cargo boats immortalised by Neil Munro in his *Para Handy* books). A sea captain from Mull told me that the *Ballisto*, loaded with coal, drove up onto rocks on the island's west side and was a total loss; but, eager to salvage the coal, the owners sent another puffer to remove it. For a reason that was never fully explained, the 'rescue' puffer sank as well and ended up sitting on top of the *Ballisto*. Neither the coal nor the boats was saved; and for years, before winter gales finally smashed both hulls to pieces, the mast of one of them stuck out of the water as a grim warning to mariners to keep well clear.

18

CORRYVRECKAN – GALE IN LOCH
CRAIGNISH – CRINAN CANAL

The Basin - Crinan Canal

High water was about mid-morning in the Sound of Mull, and I sailed out on the ebb past the grim, forbidding ramparts of the MacLean stronghold of Duart Castle and through the tide-raked gap between Mull and the island of Lismore into the Firth of Lorne. Away from the lee of the Morvern shore, the wind was stronger than it had appeared, and in the Firth of Lorne a fresh north-easterly drove *Halcyon* along at a cracking seven knots, shooting up to ten knots when I tore past the attractive little lighthouse of Fladda and was caught up in the strong ebb pouring through the Sound of Luing (Ling).

The Sound flows between the Island of Luing on its east side and the islands Lunga and Scarba on the west, and the islands are noted for having arguably the nastiest stretches of water in the west of Scotland. Between the north end of Scarba and Lunga is the Grey Dogs channel, less than a cable (185 metres) wide, where the tide runs at eight knots and even the fishermen fear it. But it is the whirlpool in the Gulf of Corryvreckan, between Scarba and Jura, that for centuries has provoked fear among mariners, and when I sailed past the entrance to the Gulf I was relieved that the ebb was pushing me away and not sucking me into it.

It was not, though, called the Great Race for nothing. The incredible volume of turbulent water that poured through the Gulf with the flood and extended several miles out into the sea on the western side, returned with the ebb, and its arrival off the eastern tip of Scarba coincided with mine. It was a very bumpy ride through the tide rip and I felt powerless when *Halcyon* was spun round in a circle by the eddies, but once I had managed to break free I ditched my vow to use the engine whenever the wind was on the nose and enjoyed a spirited beat up Loch Craignish, with the intention of staying the night in a sheltered anchorage called the Lagoon, hidden away between two small islands and the Craignish peninsula.

It was not a moment too soon. I had hardly dropped anchor and written up my log when the sky darkened and a full gale screamed out of the west as if it were the ending of the world. *Halcyon* careered backwards to the full extent of the chain and immediately an alarm went off. The anchor was dragging!

I moved forward under engine, cranked in as much chain as I could, let go the anchor again, running out the full fifty metres, and hung the angel on it. It held, and I went below to make coffee. But the gale got steadily worse, and when I stuck my hand-held wind speed indicator out of the hatch, the scale was exceeding force eight and, with a bang, the revolving bit disintegrated and blew away, so I never did know the true strength of the wind.

The strain was too much for the anchor and once more the alarm went off. On deck it was a frightening sight. Boats on nearby moorings were crashing heavily into the waves; there was so much salt spray in the air it made my eyes water and it was difficult to see. I had to find shelter, and quickly, but it was easier said than done. Each time I lifted the anchor off the bottom the wind slewed *Halcyon* round and drove her towards the moored boats, and I had to rush back to the cockpit to regain control. In the end it was the autopilot that saved the day.

With a course set to keep the bow into wind and with just enough revs on the engine to move forward very slowly, I furiously cranked the chain in and secured the anchor. Out in Loch Craignish it was bedlam. An alarming sea had built up and I waited for a smooth before I dare turn and run before the wind, hoping I might be able get alongside a pontoon at Ardfern Yacht Centre at the head of the loch. It was like sailing on an ocean. One minute I was staring down into a trough and the next the bow was high in the air and all I could see ahead of me was a wall of water.

I realised that trying to get alongside a pontoon at Ardfern would be difficult if not highly dangerous, and my only hope was to make for the lee of Eilean Righ (the King's Island) a long narrow island in the middle of the loch. The wind was absolutely screeching through the rigging, and the seas so high that trying to judge how close I was to the island was tricky, and to make sure I was well clear of off-lying rocks I went way beyond it, but that brought me close to the mainland shore.

It meant I had to turn to starboard without waiting for a smooth patch among the seas, and as soon as I put the helm hard down a steep sea rolled *Halcyon* onto her side in a trough and I thought she was turning over. She struggled to get upright, but another wave broke over her, and fearing the end, I unclipped my lifeline ready to jump into the sea. But, miracle of miracles, brave *Halcyon* righted herself, threw the water off her decks, and we were round and heading up the east side of Eilean Righ.

There had been an awful crash of pans and the sound of breaking of glass down below when *Halcyon* went over, but there was no time to inspect the damage – the strength of the wind was incredible and it needed every bit of power the engine could muster to push against it.

At first the narrow channel between Eilean Righ and the mainland appeared to be blocked with fish-farm cages, and my heart sank, but as I drew closer I could see a jetty on the island in a tiny bay and steered for it. It was as though I had sailed into another world! All around the island I could still hear the wind howling, yet by the jetty not a tree moved, and hardly able to believe my luck I sounded into the bay and dropped anchor in three metres.

The inside of the cabin was chaotic. Wine and whisky glasses had been flung out of a locker and smashed to pieces, every pan in the galley together with the kettle, the meths bottle, washing up liquid, plates, cups, cutlery, potatoes, cartons of long-life milk, onions and carrots, were all over the bunks and the floor, and even in the fore cabin. The starboard bunk cushions had been flung onto the port bunk and were neatly bonded together with strawberry jam and bits of glass from a broken jar. Charts, dividers, logbook, Reeds Almanac, pilot books, reading books, and pens and pencils were spread around like confetti.

Mercifully, all the glasses on the paraffin cabin lamps had survived. Sir Francis Chichester was supposed to have designed the lamps, and he would have known a thing or two about boats being knocked over. *Halcyon* was unscathed apart from a bent deck stanchion, and the liferaft having shifted on its wooden cradle.

Never, in all my years of sailing, had I experienced such unusually violent conditions in a Scottish sea loch, but the important thing was that we were safe, and the thanksgiving dram tasted just as good out of a plastic mug. It took a long time to clean up the debris and track down every splinter of glass, and I was so tired I forgot about making a meal, fell into my sleeping bag and had a horrible dream that *Halcyon* was floating upside down and I was trapped inside the hull.

The gale blew throughout the following day, and in between catching up on odd jobs I finished reading Joshua Slocum's *Sailing Alone Around the World*. What a remarkable achievement, but what a sad and lonely man he was following the death of his first wife, who loved the sea and sailing as much he did.

Feeling down in the dumps after reading about Slocum's misfortune, I found light relief in Neil Munro's *Para Handy Tales*, the highly amusing adventures of the incorrigible captain and crew of the steam puffer *Vital Spark*. Called 'puffers' because the early designs of engine puffed smoke out of the funnels in short bursts, the little cargo boats were the lifeline of the remote coastal and island communities in the west of Scotland for many years.

When I was at Ardnamurchan lighthouse it was a puffer that brought our coal. Being flat-bottomed, it was able to dry out on the sand in a little bay near the lighthouse, and as soon as the tide went out the keepers feverishly helped the crew to shovel the coal into a large iron bucket in the hold, which was then hoisted by the boat's steam-winch and tipped into a farm trailer hired to cart the coal to the lighthouse. The job had to be completed before the tide came in again.

The stories of the mythical *Vital Spark* were first serialised in a Glasgow newspaper, and later the stories were the basis of the BBC television series *The Vital Spark*. Not realising how popular the tales would turn out to be, the BBC failed to preserve the original six episodes, filmed in 1959–60. The amusing *Para Handy* stories were ideal for escaping from the anxiety of the weather, but eventually I had to come down to earth and face an awkward dilemma. From Eilean Righ my preferred route back to the Clyde was down the Sound of Jura and back round the Mull of Kintyre; but Clyde Coastguard was gloomily forecasting several days of strong wind, and BBC Radio Scotland's lady forecaster confirmed it.

If I went for the Mull I might be marooned in Jura or Gigha for days, or even weeks, waiting for a weather window; whereas, only about four miles from where I was anchored was Crinan harbour and the entrance to the nine-mile-long Crinan Canal, which would take me into Loch Fyne and so back to the Clyde.

The disadvantage of the canal was that I would need help with the mooring warps and also, with a few exceptions, the operating of the locks and sluices had to be carried out by a yacht's crew, and I did not have any. I waited for the late-night forecast in the hope that there would be a change for the better and I could go round the Mull, but the strong wind alert had increased to a gale warning. The message was clear. I should get help and go through the canal!

It was a wild night and I hardly slept, but the howling wind had eased when I got up to switch off the anchor light and stick my head out of the hatch to check the weather. The trees on the mainland were still swaying vigorously, and waves were breaking against the fish-farm cages, but the gale had lost its sting and I made up my mind to leave after breakfast. With every moveable item in the cabin well battened down, I hauled anchor and motored out of the bay.

Immediately I was back in the world of wild wind and breaking seas, though it was nowhere near as ferocious as the day I had been blasted down the loch. Butting into the seas and sending up clouds of spray, *Halcyon* ploughed steadily along between the mainland and Eilean Righ and Eilean Macaskin, surged round the grassy-topped Eilean Coinean (rabbit island) and rolled across Loch Crinan to the entrance of the canal.

I had timed it perfectly. As I arrived, a fishing boat was pulling out of the sea lock and the lock-keeper waved me in and secured my warps. The creaking gates closed behind me, the sluices squirted thousands of gallons of water, and *Halcyon* rose little by little until the water was level with the lock gates of the inner basin. I paid my dues, and all within an hour of leaving Eilean Righ I was through into the Crinan Canal and tied up against a stone quay.

There was hardly any wind, no seas, no tides and only the sound of herring gulls squabbling over scraps on the towpath; yet below me on Loch Crinan the sea was lathered in whitecaps and the fishing boat that was leaving the sea lock as I arrived was crashing heavily into the swell. Keen sailor though I was, there were times when I appreciated a break from the hassle of the UK's deteriorating climate, and for once I had some sympathy for the crew of the *Vital Spark*, who in the television series sang:

> *The Crinan Canal for me*
> *I don't like the wild raging sea*
> *Them big foamin' breakers*
> *Wad gie ye the shakers*
> *The Crinan Canal for me.*

But somehow I had to find two volunteers who would help me through the canal. Getting the first one was easy: I phoned my wife and she said she would drive up from our home on the edge of the Clyde right away. She had crewed and cooked for me aboard a ketch when we operated skippered charters out of Oban, but had suffered a number of severe frights in bad weather in the Hebrides, and as far as she was concerned the word 'boat' was a now a four-letter obscenity. She would come only on the understanding that as soon as we reached Ardrishaig at the Loch Fyne end of the canal, she would be out of *Halcyon* and away back home. It was the helpful lady lock-keeper at Crinan who found me my second crew in the form of Hughie Kirk, an ex-Scot's Guardsman who was putting his retirement to good use hiring his services as a canal pilot.

His knowledge of boats did not stray much beyond having made a passage on a troopship; but he had been a colonel's batman and, as I was soon to find out, was meticulous in everything he did and handled the locks with military precision. The only snag was, this being a Saturday, he was booked up all weekend and could not help until 9 a.m. Monday morning.

It was frustrating, but when my wife, Jean, arrived later that evening it was a good opportunity to use her car and spend some time discovering the delights of the picturesque shoreline of nearby Loch Fyne, Scotland's mightiest sea loch.

19

NEIL MUNRO'S ISOLATION – THE *WAVERLEY* – HOME FROM THE SEA

With a length of over forty miles, Loch Fyne is the longest loch, and through its centuries-old association with herring fishing ranks among the most important of the many sea lochs that are linked to the great River Clyde. The days of the traditional, locally caught Loch Fyne kippers are long gone, but the old communities are still there, and at the head of the loch is the charming little town of Inveraray. For centuries it has been in the unrelenting grip of a succession of Dukes of Argyll, the chiefs of the Clan Campbell; and it was one of the dukes who unwittingly became the nation's first 'Nimby' (Not in my back yard) when in 1745, having decided to build himself a fine new castle, he objected to the town being close to the chosen site and had it knocked down.

Pennant, who travelled extensively in the Highlands during that time, described the old town as 'composed of wretched hovels'. The Duke greatly improved the living conditions by building his new town close to edge of Loch Fyne, so he did the locals a favour and today Inveraray kneels submissively at the doorstep of his flamboyant castle. It was once the county town of Argyll, before the bureaucrats bundled the administration of the Highlands into more convenient pigeonholes; but now, starved of status and a purpose, the town is kept alive by tourism.

We had our hearts set on a guided tour of the Duke's turreted pile, but it appeared to be on the itinerary of every coach operator in the world and it was impossible to get near the door. Neil Munro, the author of the *Para Handy* stories, was born in Inveraray and I was amazed that there was nothing, anywhere that I could see, that boasted the town's connection with him. When we had lunch in a cafe and I mentioned it to the owner, he apologetically directed us to a lonely hill, seven miles outside the town, where someone had erected a stone obelisk in Munro's memory. A chiselled inscription read simply 'Neil Munro 1863–1930', and I could not help wondering if, at some time, Munro had caricatured a Duke of Argyll in one of his stories and was paying the price in isolation.

I had arranged to meet Hughie, the canal pilot, on Monday morning at Dunardry locks, three miles along the canal from Crinan sea lock, and to be sure of arriving there in good time we left Crinan late on Sunday afternoon and chugged along one of the most delightful stretches of canal to be found anywhere. It had been built high above sea level, and on our left side was a wonderful panoramic view of the salt flats of the estuary of the River Add and the wide expanse of the Moine Mhor (the Great Moss) nature reserve.

We passed old-fashioned, white-painted retractable bridges, operated with slow deliberation by lock-keepers for whom time had no meaning and who, when we had gone by, went back to their picture postcard cottages with gardens filled with flowers. They could have been scenes from paintings by Constable, but this was Scotland. Wild ducks, coots and moorhens glided in and out of tiny bays choked with water lilies, and on the bank a heron stood motionless while only a beak's length away fish jumped and splashed back into the water as if taunting it. Seagulls that had fled inland from the gales looked very self-conscious as they paddled along in alien surroundings.

Our boaty nature ramble ended all too soon at Dunardry locks, where a white mist was forming over the still water of the canal, though Clyde Coastguard rather spoilt the serenity by revealing that, though the vigorous low-pressure system that had stirred up gale-force winds had veered to the north, our part of the west of Scotland could expect more strong wind and occasional showers of rain.

Contrary to the forecast, a thick mist still hung over the canal at daylight the following morning and I worried that I might be held up for another day, but when Hughie appeared at 9 a.m. he said that sometimes the canal appeared to have a weather pattern of its own and the mist would soon clear. Meantime, he explained that he would drive along in his van and open and close the lock gates and handle the sluices. All we were required to do was to motor *Halcyon* into the lock and heave the mooring warps up to him.

The mist cleared away as he had predicted, and he busied himself with opening the sluices to let the water in and pushing hard with his back against the massive wooden 'swing bars' that controlled the lock gates. Slowly but surely, Dunardry's set of five locks lifted us up to the highest reach of the canal, and thereafter it was all 'downhill' through four sets of locks and an opening road bridge at Cairnbaan, followed by four miles of pleasant chugging along a placid waterway to a final set of three locks and the sea basin at Ardrishaig on Loch Fyne.

Our canal pilot's military-style organisation had run like clockwork, and by 1 p.m. I was filling *Halcyon*'s freshwater tanks from a hose at the pontoon, while Hughie very kindly ran Jean back to Crinan for her car. It was an occasion for a change from shipboard food, and that evening we enjoyed local hospitality and a mammoth bar meal in a pub in Ardrishaig.

Ignoring all my hints, offers, bribes, promises of calm, sheltered waters, and every inducement I could think of to get her to stay with me on the last leg of my journey, Jean ran for her car after breakfast the next day and was halfway home before I had cleared the Ardrishaig sea lock and was hoisting sail in Loch Fyne. She had heard it all before! I was on my own.

She had seen the menacing bank of cloud racing in from the north, confirming the Coastguard's warning of more unsettled weather. In the middle of the loch, away from the protection of Ardrishaig, I felt the full force of a north-westerly wind that on his wind scale the 19th-century navigator Admiral Beaufort described as a 'fresh breeze', about twenty knots or force five, or in landlubber speak about twenty-five miles an hour. When the black cloud swooped in and brought fierce squalls of chilling rain it zoomed up to 'strong breeze', force six, twenty-five knots, or about thirty miles an hour, and was an unpleasant change after the relaxing weekend in the canal.

The northerly wind was bitterly cold with the rain more continuous than occasional, but not being in any particular hurry I bowled along under mizzen and jib, steering for Sgat Island lighthouse, a white dot in the distance.

Loch Fyne rules over a complex of sea lochs that link arms with the River Clyde to create a cruising area that is a sailor's dream; though, like many rulers, it has an unstable temperament and is given to wild extremes. At the bat of an eyelid the weather can change from placid smooth to a mini-tempest that kicks up short, steep seas with foaming crests and has caused many an expensive dinner ashore to be left trailing in the wake of a yacht.

It was noticeable that, while *Halcyon* surfed down Loch Fyne at six knots in a force five, a sudden squall that bounced the wind up to force six squeezed another knot out of her, and by this extraordinary jerky motion and in drenching rain we sped down the loch, past Sgat lighthouse and round Ardlamont Point into one of the best-known and most sailed routes in Scotland, Na Caoil Bhodach – the Kyles of Bute.

The island of Bute, famous for its spectacular stately home, bustling harbour town, lovely quiet walks and superb views, owes its island status to a moat-like stretch of water which separates it from the mainland and runs up both sides of the island. The ancient Gaels called the moat on the west side An Caol an Iar – the West Kyle, and on the east side An Caol an Ear – the East Kyle, though whether the name Buttock Point aptly describes the part of Bute where the island's northern tip divides the Kyles no one has been brave enough to comment on!

When I gybed round Ardlamont Point buoy into West Kyle, the wind was blanketed by the land and with barely enough movement to maintain steerage way, I dropped the sails and used the engine to push *Halcyon* towards the coastal communities of Kames and Tighnabruich (house on the hill), and round Buttock Point to the entrance of East Kyle.

At first the tiny Burnt Islands strewn across the Kyle seem to block progress, until a glance at the chart reveals two buoyed channels laid out with the international buoyage system of red buoys to port (left) and green to starboard (right) in the direction of the flow of the flood tide. Sailing from west to east is straightforward, but some confusion can arise among skippers new to the area who are nearing the Burnt Islands channels from the north end of East Kyle for the first time, believing they have the flood with them, and are mystified to discover that not only do the channel buoys appear to have been laid the wrong way round with the green buoys on the left and red buoys on the right, but a tidal stream is doing its best to push their boat backwards, sometimes running at three knots.

The scale of the Admiralty Tide Atlas for the West of Scotland is too small to be of any use in the Kyles, but the cause of the mystification is that although the flood tide runs up both sides of Bute, the streams do not meet at the north of the island as might be expected. The flood stream in West Kyle gallops ahead and flows round the top, goes through the Burnt Islands channels and heads down East Kyle for about a mile or so until it meets the slower East Kyle flood stream heading north. Perhaps overwhelmed by the beauty of the Kyles, visiting mariners some-times fail to interpret this tidal oddity in the sailing directions, and in the summer months the surrounding hills have been known to echo with the crunch of keels striking rocks when a helmsman has strayed on the wrong side of a buoy.

All the way up West Kyle, the wind had been light and the rain patchy, but in East Kyle the venturi effect of the northerly wind being squeezed between the hills created incredibly violent squalls that laid *Halcyon* right over under bare poles and, completely helpless, there was nothing I could do about it except hang on to the tiller. With the squalls, the raindrops drove into me like bullets, and I could barely make out the ferry that ran between Colintraive and Bute, but luckily the skipper had seen me and obligingly waited until I had passed.

There was absolutely no shelter nor respite from the wind until I reached the end of East Kyle and got away from the hills, and feeling sorely in need of a mug of coffee and a hot meal I made for Bute's main harbour, Rothesay, in company with the old paddle steamer *Waverley*. When she was secured to the pier I crept round her stern and tied up alongside a yacht pontoon in the harbour. Being so close to such a historic ship was a good chance to get a few photographs and, grabbing my cameras, I raced up to the pier.

'Are you coming aboard?' shouted the mate, as the crew started to remove the gangplank.

'I might be,' I laughed. 'Where are you going?'

'We're going up the Kyles to Tighnabruich, then back to Rothesay,' replied the mate. 'It's our last trip of the season. Make your mind up quick.'

It was a chance too good to miss and, forgetting I was wet and cold and longing for a hot drink, I ran up the gangplank and stepped onto the deck of the last seagoing paddle steamer in the world. With three blasts on her siren to indicate she was going astern, the old ship backed away from the pier, then turned in a wide arc and, with a loud clattering from the paddles enclosed in ornate boxes on either side of the hull, rushed forward at an astonishing speed.

Shivering with cold, I dived below to the refreshment bar for coffee and a hot meal, and by the time I had thawed out and returned on deck I had missed the run back up East Kyle and the captain was lining up the bow to go through the narrow buoyed channel at the Burnt Islands. The lively gusts of wind that had bowled *Halcyon* onto her side were still roaring down from the hills, but the passengers crowding the deck clung onto the side rails or the seats, determined not to miss a moment of the mountain scenery and the experience of the old *Waverley* weaving its way between the islands.

Steaming through a narrow channel between the top of the Isle of Bute and the mainland, the ship pulled alongside an old wooden pier at Tighnabruich, in much the same way as passenger steam ships had been doing for centuries among the Highlands and Islands before progress in the form of trains and buses finished them off. But what trains and buses could never do was replace the magic and romance of ships, and the survival and the enormous popularity of the *Waverley* had proved that.

A muffled voice on a loudspeaker announced that the *Waverley* would be at the pier for an hour and that passengers could go ashore. Most of them swarmed off the pier, eager to sample the fleshpots of Tighnabruich – a few tearooms, a pub, a giftshop and a lifeboat station – but having experienced enough of the Kyles of Bute weather for that day, I stayed aboard, wandered round the engine room and the rest of the ship, and finally came to rest in the refreshment bar where, with a mug of hot coffee to hand, I settled into a corner and read a brochure about the *Waverley*.

Over 73 metres long, weighing in at nearly 700 tonnes, and driven by a steam engine fuelled by heavy oil, the ship had been built in 1947 to replace the original *Waverley* that was destroyed during the evacuation of troops at Dunkirk in 1940. For years the elegant little paddle steamer, with its familiar twin red funnels with white and black bands at the top, ran excursions around the sea lochs of the Clyde, but in 1974 the operating company ran out of funds and the world's last seagoing paddle steamer might have ended her days being sold for scrap, had it not been for the members of the Paddle Steamer Preservation Society. They bought the *Waverley* for £1, but the price included a stack of almost insurmountable problems that took many years and a lot of supporters' cash to overcome. The year 2003 saw the completion of a major restoration project when *Waverley* was returned to her original 1940s style, and since then she has been a familiar sight not only on the Clyde but as far away as the Thames and the south coast of England.

When the time came to leave Tighnabruich before the ship was laid up for the winter, there were blasts from the ship's siren and so many tearful waves and hugs and kisses from the shore staff that even a heavy shower of rain did little to dampen the emotion. It felt like an emigrant ship outward bound for the New World, but it was really a gesture of the immense affection people had for the lovely old *Waverley*.

With a remarkable service speed of fourteen knots, the paddles clattered us back down East Kyle in a fraction of the time it had taken me in *Halcyon*, and when she departed from Rothesay there was more waving from well-wishers.

Standing on *Halcyon's* foredeck I was one of them, thrilled that I had sailed on a ship that was a piece of living history. Too tired to make a meal, I bought fish and chips in Rothesay and ate them while wrapped up in my sleeping bag, snug alongside the cabin stove, with the rain drumming against the skylight. I was at peace with the world.

Rothesay was only ten miles from my home mooring, and the log showed I had sailed over a thousand miles since I left Fairlie; but I searched for any excuse to postpone the end of my cruise, and for once the weather was on my side. During the night it conveniently deteriorated, and by breakfast it was blowing a howler and raining hard. I told myself that no prudent sailor would ever consider putting to sea in such conditions, and with a clear conscience shouldered my rucksack and caught a bus to have a walk around the grounds of Mount Stuart, the Marquess of Bute's stately home in the south of the island.

The bus was packed with glum-faced tourists dripping rainwater over the seats, and a harassed mother was trying to control her unruly boy of about five years old.

'I'm gonna to be sick!' wailed the child as the bus left the town and was driving along a leafy country lane.

'Driver, stop ya bus,' yelled the boy's mother. 'Ma wee boy's gonna be sick.'

With a silent curse the driver pulled into a lay-by and the mother hurriedly bundled her offspring down the steps.

'Well, go on then, be sick!' she ordered.

'I'm no wantin' tae be sick noo. I'm needin' tae pee,' wailed the monster.

Mother fumbled for his willy, pointed it at the bus wheel and the child duly performed.

'It's a guid job he was no wantin' to dae anythin' else,' said the driver despairingly when the pee splashed up the steps of the bus and dribbled round his feet, but the mother just glared at him. We reached Mount Stuart without any more hold-ups, and making sure that mother and child headed off in the opposite direction to the one I was taking, I wandered round the gardens and outhouses.

Rebuilt in 1878 after a disastrous fire destroyed the original building, Mount Stuart was quite an imposing stately home, but in the rain the red sandstone building looked positively dismal. I joined a tour of the house, and an enthusiastic guide with a tremendous sense of humour helped to drive away the damp atmosphere with a fascinating talk that brought alive the history of Mount Stuart and the Crichton-Stuart family who had lived on Bute since the 13th century.

Resisting the tempting aromas drifting up from the old kitchen that had been turned into a smart tearoom, I found a deserted summerhouse in the grounds and spread out my flask of tea and corned beef sandwiches on a bench. It was still windy, but the rain had eased off and laser beams of sunlight cascaded through the clouds, lighting up individual trees as though they had been set ablaze.

It was too good a day to be wasted sitting on a bus, and I walked back to Rothesay along a quiet back road that went by lovely Loch Ascog and miles of neatly fenced green fields.

With promises of a better day to come, and even talk of sunshine, it was as if the evening forecaster on BBC Radio Scotland was determined I should have good weather for the last day of my cruise, and even the normally strait-laced duty radio operators at Clyde Coastguard sounded pleased that the weather was about to make a rapid improvement. There would be no cheering crowds, brass bands, and tugs squirting their fire hoses into the air when I arrived home, only my wife Jean and my dog would be waiting to greet 'the sailor home from the sea'; but before settling in for the night I scrubbed *Halcyon's* decks and washed the salt stains off the varnish work in the approved fashion of a sailing ship returning home after a voyage.

After experiencing so much wind and rain, it was a tremendous relief when I peered out of the hatch the next day and saw streaks of blue sky and a hazy sun, and for the first time for many days I breakfasted in the cockpit. To use up as much perishable food as possible, I cooked an unusually gargantuan breakfast of bacon, eggs, sausages, mushrooms, black pudding and tomatoes, but my stomach soon told me that it was not the wisest of things to have done, and I was forced to sit for a while to digest it before I could muster the energy to cast off and sail out of Rothesay Bay into the Clyde.

There was a south-westerly breeze, and to celebrate the final run I hoisted every stitch of canvas I could find, including the topsail, which I very rarely used. With a heavy five-metre-long boom and a four-metre gaff to handle when hoisting the main sail, the topsail was normally more than I could cope with on my own, but this time it was hauled up to the masthead and, with her cream hull and red sails,

Halcyon must have looked exceptionally attractive in the sun. Passing motor yachts altered course and came close so that those on board could take photographs.

To my surprise, as I was about to cross the main shipping channel I had to wait until a nuclear submarine, inbound from the sea, had passed on its way up the Clyde to the submarine base at Faslane. It was accompanied by the usual posse of fast police launches, and it was such a coincidence I wondered if it might be the same submarine that had held me up at the start of my voyage and now, like me, was nearing the end of it.

It was a lovely day, and when the flotilla had gone *Halcyon* seemed to soar over the seas, dipping her bow into the wash of the submarine and rolling gently in the tidal swell. At first the long mass of Great Cumbrae Island was lost against the mainland and hard to distinguish, but gradually it began to form its own identity, with green fields, trees, farmhouses, rocky bays and, when we rounded its northern tip, the ferry that ran back and forth from Cumbrae to Largs.

On we sailed, past Largs Marina and Fairlie Marina and finally to my mooring in Fairlie Bay, only a few metres away from the now demolished site of Fife's yard, where the Americas Cup challengers *Shamrock I* and *Shamrock III* were designed for Sir Thomas Lipton, and where many equally famous yachts were built.

Easing the sails, I rounded up alongside the mooring, dropped the loop of the pickup rope over the samson post, and *Halcyon* drifted back with the tide until the chain held her.

The ghost of John Jago had brought his 'dream ship' safely home after a memorable Hebridean adventure. It was the perfect ending.